City Breaks in Moscow and Leningrad

REG BUTLER

In Association with

CITYBREAKS

SETTLE PRESS (WIGMORE)
HIPPOCRENE BOOKS INC.

While every reasonable care has been taken by the
author and publisher in presenting the information in
this book, no responsibility can be taken by them or by
Thomson Holidays for any inaccuracies. Information and
prices were correct at time of printing.

Texts and maps © 1989 Reg Butler
All rights reserved. No part of this publication may be
reproduced or transmitted in any form or by any means
without permission.
First published by Settle Press (Wigmore)
32 Savile Row
London W1X 1AG

ISBN (Paperback) 0 907070 53 1

Published in United States by
Hippocrene Books Inc
171 Madison Avenue, New York
ISBN 0-87052-735-5

Printed by Villiers Publications Ltd
26a Shepherds Hill, London N6 5AH
Covers by Thumb Design Partnership
City plans by Mary Butler

Foreword

As Britain's leading short breaks specialist, we clearly recognise the need for detailed information and guidance for you, the would-be traveller. Yet a Citybreak is about more than museum opening times and table d'hôte tariffs, it's a quite sudden and easy submersion in the continental lifestyle – albeit for only a few days.

We were therefore particularly delighted to be able to work with Reg Butler and Settle Press on the City Breaks series. Reg Butler has provided for us a very readable book packed not only with important practical information but with colourful observations in a personal style that captures the very essence of your City Break city.

As well as City Breaks in Moscow and Leningrad, you will find on the bookshelves City Breaks in Paris, Amsterdam, Rome, Florence and Venice, and of course Thomson operate to 18 cities in Europe and the Americas from departure points across the UK.

We're sure you'll find this book invaluable in planning your short break in Moscow and Leningrad.

THOMSON CITYBREAKS

Contents

Page

1. **RUSSIAN CITYBREAK**
   1.1 Introducing Russia 5
   1.2 Where Tourism is different 7
   1.3 Your City Break hotel 10
   1.4 At your Service 11
   1.5 Public Transport and Sightseeing 14
   1.6 Russian Sunday 17
   1.7 Shopping 19
   1.8 Russian Cuisine 21
   1.9 Nightlife 23
   1.10 Learn Russian ABC 25

2. **MOSCOW**
   2.1 Welcome to Moscow 27
   2.2 Finding your way round Moscow 30
   2.3 Red Square 31
   2.4 Inside the Kremlin 35
   2.5 The Rest of Basic Moscow 41
   2.6 A stroll down Gorky Street 44
   2.7 Take a Trip 46
   2.8 Selection of Museums & Galleries 48
   2.9 Shopping 53
   2.10 Eating out in Moscow 54
   2.11 Moscow by night 55

3. **LENINGRAD**
   3.1 Window on the West 57
   3.2 Getting your bearings 61
   3.3 Basic Leningrad 62
   3.4 Stroll along Nevsky Prospekt 69
   3.5 Take a trip 71
   3.6 What else to see in Leningrad 73
   3.7 Shopping 76
   3.8 Eating out in Leningrad 77
   3.9 Leningrad by Night 78

Maps

Metro 15
Moscow 28–29
Red Square 32
Leningrad 58–59

Chapter One

1.1 Introducing Russia

Fifteen republics together make up the USSR. Each takes pride in its individual culture and language – as different from one another as, say, Egypt is from Norway.

Largest of these republics is the Russian Soviet Federal Socialist Republic – RSFSR or Russia for short – which covers three-quarters of the Soviet Union. Russia crosses 11 time zones, from the Polish border to the Pacific Coast, including Siberia and the Far East territories. The other republics are spread around the edges of that Russian heartland.

This enormous area of Russia is itself sub-divided into 16 autonomous republics – making up the 'Federation' – which each have their own state authority, capital, emblem and flag. Fifty different languages are spoken in areas where Russian is the first foreign language to be taught in schools.

The two largest cities of the Soviet Union are Moscow and Leningrad which have alternated as the Russian capital. As the centres of political activity, administration, industry, science and higher education, they are sophisticated cities with a rich cultural life – museums, art galleries, theatres and concert halls. They also act as showcases of Soviet folklore, music, dance and peasant art.

Virtually every tour to the Soviet Union begins or ends with two or three nights in Moscow or Leningrad, which also are popular destinations for city breaks of three to seven nights. On a one week holiday, the two cities can easily be linked by rail. Both cities offer a great range of sightseeing potential, keeping you hectically occupied for three or four days. Stay longer, and you have more time to indulge in your special interests, or to get a deeper understanding of the Soviet life-style.

Much of the fascination comes from seeing how the other political half of the world lives. You'll be shown around by Intourist guides with evocative Russian names like Natasha, Olga and Tanya: well-educated young ladies with remarkable fluency in English.

In line with Gorbachev's policy of *glasnost* – openness –

you will probably find them quite ready to talk about subjects which formerly were rather embarrassing: the Stalin purges, high level corruption, or the poor quality of many consumer products. But, just as in any other country, the guides will mainly show you the sunny side of life. Their business is tourism, not politics. Most visitors to Russia are looking for an enjoyable holiday, not for a fevered debate on socialism versus capitalism.

Both cities offer many pleasant surprises. Litter, graffiti and smog are virtually unknown. There are almost no factories near the city centres. Heating systems are non-polluting, based entirely on natural gas. Road traffic is relatively light by Western standards – thanks especially to the super efficient and incredibly cheap Metro systems. You can stay a week without seeing a traffic jam.

When to go?

Russia is a year-round destination. Leningrad and Moscow are well geared to the famous Russian winter. Snow-capped palaces and churches, children on toboggans, and soldiers in furry hats – they all have a picture-book charm. Pavements are constantly swept clear by cube-shaped ladies with witches' brooms, leaving not a snow-flake unturned.

Double glazing and central heating ensure comfort in hotels, museums and theatres. Be prepared to peel off outer layers of clothing. The wearing of an overcoat in a museum or gallery is regarded as 'uncultured', and every public place is equipped with well-organised cloakrooms. Canvas overshoes are provided in the palaces, to protect polished floors.

The crisp weather is invigorating. Muscovites go swimming in the open-air heated Baths. Paths in Gorky Park are flooded for skating, with loudspeaker music till 11 p.m. Ice skates can be hired. A 'Russian Winter Festival' is held in the grounds of the USSR Exhibition of Economic Achievements (VDNKh) from 25 December to 5 January, with concerts, folklore shows and troika sleigh rides.

A similar seasonal event is held in Leningrad, with dances around a New Year tree, hot pancakes with caviar, and the essential troika rides. Leningrad also arranges a Farewell to the Russian Winter – 19 February to 5 March – with folklore festivities.

Wintertime, you'll stand a much better chance of seeing the top ballet and opera stars, when they're playing their home season. During summer months, world-famed companies can disappear on international tours. But always there are other Soviet companies to take their place on stage. Moscow and Leningrad are never 'off-season'!

1.2 Where Tourism is 'Different'

Visas, Customs Regulations, Money and Photography

Compared with travel in the Western world, tourism in the Soviet Union is 'different'. Some of the differences may seem irritating. But there's no way they are going to change their system. It's best just to relax, and accept the differences as part of the fascination: seeing how things tick in Eastern Europe.

Remember that, on entering the Soviet Union, you become subject to the laws of a State with a political and judicial system different from that of the western world. Certain activities which are legal in the West are subject to severe penalties – for example, the unofficial exchange of foreign currency.

Here are some of the differences to expect, and the ground-rules:

Visas

Nobody can enter the Soviet Union without a valid visa, which is normally issued 10-12 days prior to departure. Your tour operator will advise you of the procedure.

It's your own responsibility to check that your visa has been correctly completed by the authorities. If you are travelling with children under 16 years who are included on your passport check that their names appear on the visas as well as your own.

The visa is a separate piece of paper *not* stamped in your passport. Likewise, your passport will not be stamped on arrival or departure.

Travelling within the USSR

If you intend to visit relatives in the Soviet Union, make this quite clear to your tour representative when you arrive. For individual travel outside Moscow, a visa is required, and should be arranged through Intourist.

Arrival in USSR

Flight time from London to Moscow or Leningrad is just under 4 hours. Moscow time is ahead of London by 3 hours.

On arrival in the terminal you proceed through Health and Immigration Control, for which you require your passport and visa. The Immigration Officer will return your passport and part of the visa, which must be retained until departure. It is advisable if you have recently been travelling in other countries, especially Asia or Africa, to check the health regulations.

Collect your luggage and proceed through Customs. This is a lengthy operation, and can take up to 1½ hours.

7

Currency and Customs Regulations

All foreign currency in Travellers' Cheques and banknotes, and all valuables taken into the USSR, must be declared on a Customs Declaration Form.

There is no limit upon the amount of foreign currency brought into the USSR but import or export of roubles is not permitted. Likewise, no letters, messages, money packages or material of any kind should be carried into or out of the USSR on behalf of third parties, unless you have prior permission from the Soviet authorities.

Complete the Declaration Form in capitals with black ink. Where an answer is negative, write NONE. The form is examined and stamped by the Soviet Customs officer, and kept by you until departure.

The control system is rounded off as you leave the country. On departure, you fill out another Declaration Form, and details are compared with those on the original form. Keep receipts for major purchases, particularly high-value furs, jewellery or cameras. All the paperwork is designed to block black-market deals, or the illicit export of valuables. For the law-abiding tourist, there's nothing to worry about.

Money & Banking

The currency unit in the USSR is the Rouble. Depending on exchange fluctuations in the Western world, a rouble equals about £1 sterling or US $1.70.

One rouble = 100 kopeks. So a kopek equals one English penny, or about two US cents.

12p50 means 12 roubles 50 kopeks. (The 'p' is really the Russian 'r', short for rouble.)

Coins: 1, 2, 3, 5, 10, 15, 20, 50 kopeks
Notes: 1, 3, 5, 10, 25, 50, 100 Roubles

Changing Money

Normally, you need to change only a modest sum into roubles – like £10 or US $20 per person. The reason is that you are required to pay for most goods and services with hard currency – *not* roubles. Western currency is needed for optional excursions, theatre tickets, and purchases in the special 'Beriozka' shops. Hotels have 'currency bars' where roubles are refused. In general, you'll just need roubles for some incidental drinks, snacks, postcards and stamps, public transport, minor souvenirs or books.

Money should be changed *only* at an official exchange bureau. You may be approached by black marketeers who offer fantastic rates. Such dealings are quite illegal. Don't risk spoiling your holiday.

For your basic supply of roubles, hotel currency exchange desks are open much longer than banks, and are easier to deal with. The standard commission charge on

Traveller Cheques is 50 kopek – 50p – for *each cheque*. It is advisable to take cheques issued by the main High Street or international banks, since those of lesser-known banks are sometimes not accepted. Eurocheques are NOT yet widely accepted.

Your currency declaration form is *always* needed to exchange money. Keep it in your wallet or purse – not in your passport, which mostly stays with hotel reception. The cashier will note on it the amount exchanged, and will give you a currency exchange receipt. Keep this receipt, so that any surplus roubles on departure can be reconverted back to hard currency. However, try to use up all roubles before reaching the airport, as there is sometimes a long queue at the airport exchange desk. Use any final kopeks for a farewell drink, or keep them as souvenirs.

You can obtain roubles against credit cards, such as American Express, Eurocard/Access/Mastercard, Diners' Club and Visa. However, roubles received against credit cards cannot be converted back, and should all be spent in the USSR.

Because so many tourist transactions in USSR are made in hard currency, take plenty of *cash* in smaller-denomination banknotes and a range of coinage, including £1 and 50p coins which are particularly useful in hotel currency bars. Dollar bills, especially singles, are ideal. All bank notes should be clean and fairly new, otherwise you risk them not being accepted as valid currency. Scottish pound notes are not acceptable.

Photography

There is plenty to photograph in the Soviet Union, and you should take *more than enough* film. It's often impossible to obtain the particular films you would use at home.

Note: X-ray equipment which could affect your films is often used at Soviet airports. Pack them separately, so that you can by-pass the machines.

The regulations on photography for foreigners are as follows:

1. Photographs may be taken or sketches made of architectural monuments, buildings of cultural instructional interest, medical establishments, theatres, museums, parks of culture and rest, of stadiums, streets, squares and dwelling houses, throughout the territory of the USSR, except at points or places which foreigners are forbidden to visit. The same applies to views and landscapes, provided none of the items listed below in paragraph 3 are in the background.

2. On individual occasions, provided permission has been given by the administration of the establishment or organization in question, photographs may be taken or

sketches made inside factories engaged in civil production, railway stations, aerodromes, river ports and Government buildings.

3. Photography or sketching is forbidden:

(a) In the 25 kilometres frontier strip, except for those points and places which are not closed to visits by foreigners, where they may photograph objects listed in paragraph (1) above.

(b) Of all views of military equipment or arms, of all military objects, establishments and fuel stores.

(c) Of naval ports, hydro-electric installations (sluices, dams, barrages, pumping stations), of railway junctions, tunnels, railway and road bridges, on the platform of many railway and metro stations.

(d) Of industrial undertakings, of scientific research institutes, constructional bureaux, laboratories, electricity stations, radio beacons, radio stations, telephone and telegraphic stations.

(e) From aircraft flying over the Territory of the USSR, and also ground photography while on your flight and at all Russian airports.

N.B. It is advisable to keep cameras packed inside your hand baggage to avoid any difficulty at airports.

1.3 Your City Break Hotel

It sounds incredible, but nobody knows at which hotel they'll stay – only the category – until the individual or group is met on arrival by the tour representative. There is no advance choice on which hotel will be used. Essentially there is a chronic shortage of hotel rooms, as the Five Year Plans did not anticipate such a boom in tourism. Each day's arrivals are fed into the Intourist computer, and the software decides where each group will be allocated. It's a Lucky Dip system, and there's no point in getting steamed up about it.

On arrival at the designated hotel, you hand over passport with visa to reception, who normally hold it until you leave. It's quite safe, no need to panic.

You'll be given a 'key card'. The first digit indicates the floor, and the remainder is your room number. A 'floor lady' on each floor keeps the keys, and generally looks after you. She can be very helpful. If anything goes wrong in your bedroom, like a light bulb not working, she'll get it fixed. When you go out, leave your hotel key with her. (Some hotels are now following the Western system of holding keys at the Hall Porter's desk.)

Always keep the key card with you. Hotels have doormen on duty. Show your key card to gain admittance. Non-residents may only enter with permission.

Also, if you go out and get lost, the key card has your

10

hotel address in Russian. Show it to a passer-by, and he can point you in the right direction.

Hotel Hints

Voltage is 220-V AC. For any electric gadgets, pack a continental two-pin adaptor plug. Travellers from North America will need a transformer.

Many hotels do not have wash-basin plugs. Russians think it's more hygienic to wash in running water. If this bothers you, pack a 'Multi-plug', which you can easily buy in the UK or USA.

Tipping? Officially it is discouraged. But if you wish to show appreciation, Western cigarettes are often welcomed.

Watch your tour operator's information board for special notices. Make a habit of checking for any new items, each time you pass.

1.4   At Your Service

What to Pack

Clothes: Russian winters are very cold, although it can be pleasant when it's sunny with sparkling snow. Hotels, museums and theatres are always well heated, so take different layers of clothes to cope with changes in temperature. A heavy winter coat, hat, scarf and gloves are essential.

Summer months can be quite warm, so cotton clothes are quite suitable. But always take at least one warm outfit, and a plastic mac.

Shoes: Aim for comfort, rather than high fashion. Many tourist locations – such as Red Square – are paved with cobbles. In winter, bring shoes or boots that are completely suitable for snow, slush and wet.

Camera films and batteries: Take *much more* of your favourite film than you think you'll need. Western brands – and even Soviet-made films – are hard to find. Carry spare batteries for electronic equipment, if only to save shopping time.

Toiletries: Take a full supply for the trip – Western brands are not available.

Other useful items: Snacks, confectionery, powdered milk for your tea, water purifying tablets.

If mosquitoes normally have you for supper, bring precautionary kit. Surrounded by water, Leningrad in July and August is firmly in the mosquito belt. There is no problem in Moscow.

Duty Free

There are 'duty free' shops at the airport on departure

from Moscow. A 'duty free' area at Leningrad airport is planned to open in April 1989. In general, if you want any duty-frees, buy them before you leave the UK departure airport or on the plane. For a tipple in your room, bring 'mixers' as well.

The allowance for each person into the Soviet Union is: half a litre of spirits or of fortified wine; and one litre of table wine.

Literature

Regular newspapers and magazines are permitted into the Soviet Union, but no pornographic publications are allowed.

News

One can feel somewhat starved of English-language news. Western newspapers are on sale at hotel kiosks, though supplies rapidly run out.

It's worth travelling with a short-wave radio, to pick up the regular on-the-hour bulletins of the BBC World Service. Reception varies according to time and location. You can usually find the BBC by fishing around these frequencies: 15070 kHz on 19-metre band; 12095 kHz on 25 metres; 9410 kHz on 31 metres.

To get Voice of America, try 9760 kHz on 31 metre band; or 6040 kHz on 49 metres.

Time

Moscow and Leningrad are normally 3 hours ahead of UK time or 8 hours ahead of East Coast USA.

Postal Services

The post office handles postal, telegraph and telephone services. Major hotels have their own branches of the post office, selling stamps and accepting telegrams until the evening. Also, wherever you buy postcards, you can usually buy stamps. In Moscow there is 24 hour service at the Central Telegraph Office at 7 Gorky Street.

Airmail postal rates to UK: postcards 35 kopeks; letters 50 kopeks. Reckon 10 to 15 days for mail to reach UK.

Telephone

Local phone calls from a house or your hotel are usually free. Calls from public telephone booths cost 2 kopeks (2X1 or 1X2). Wait for the tone and then dial your number.

For international calls, there is no direct-dial facility. You must book your phone call with your floor lady. Then you go back to your bedroom, and be prepared to wait up to an hour. International phone calls are expensive – three roubles a minute to Britain or other west European countries; nine roubles a minute to North America. The minimum charge is for three minutes at a cost of 10 roubles to the UK or 27 roubles to US or Canada. This can be paid either direct to the floor lady, or at the reception desk. In Moscow you can also make long distance calls from the Central Telegraph Office at 7 Gorky Street.

Medical Facilities

Medical treatment in the Soviet Union is free for visitors, though this is under discussion. In case of need, tell your representative or the hotel service desk, who will arrange for a doctor to visit you.

Medicines are available on prescription from the chemist at a small charge. It's worth bringing your own first-aid pack containing, for example, T.C.P. or similar liquid antiseptic, plasters, insect bite cream, travel sickness tablets and medicine for upset stomachs.

Smoking

Smoking is not permitted on public transport or in public areas, including Moscow's Red Square.

Weights and Measures

Length

1 inch	= 2.54 centimetres
1 foot	= 0.30 metres
1 mile	= 1.61 kilometres
1 centimetre	= 0.40 inches
1 metre	= 3.28 feet
1 kilometre	= 0.62 miles

Weight

1 ounce	= 28.35 grammes
1 pound	= 0.45 kilogrammes
1 gramme	= 0.035 ounces
1 kilo	= 2.205 pounds

Fluid

1 pint	= 0.57 litres
1 litre	= 1.75 pints

Clothing Sizes

Women's Dress and Suits

British	32(8)	34(10)	36(12)	38(14)	40(16)	42(18)
Continental	38	40	42	44	46	48

Men's Suits and Overcoats

British	36	38	40	42	44
Continental	46	48	50	52	54

Men's Shirts

British	14½	15	15½	16	16½	17
Continental	37	38	39	40	42	43

Women's Shoes

British	2	3	4	5	6	7	8
Continental	34	36	37	38	39	40	41

Men's Shoes

British	5	6	7	8	9	10	11
Continental	38	39	40	41	42	43	44

Climate

TEMPERATURES – midday averages (°F)

	Jan	Feb	Mar	Apr	May	Jun	Jul	Aug	Sep	Oct	Nov	Dec
MOSCOW												
High	14	19	32	43	60	67	71	68	56	44	32	17
Low	5	8	18	29	42	50	54	51	42	33	23	10
LENINGRAD												
High	19	22	32	46	59	68	70	69	60	48	35	26
Low	8	11	18	33	42	51	55	55	47	39	28	18

PRECIPITATION – monthly averages (inches)

	Jan	Feb	Mar	Apr	May	Jun	Jul	Aug	Sep	Oct	Nov	Dec
Moscow	1.9	1.8	1.9	1.7	2.1	2.7	3.2	2.5	2.2	2.2	2.2	2.2

Obviously, most of the November–March precipation is snow. The pattern for Leningrad is similar.

1.5 Public Transport and Sightseeing

The Soviet Union is outstanding for the excellence and low cost of its transport systems. Most superb of all is the Moscow Metro, inaugurated in the 1930's and copied in Leningrad and other major Soviet cities. They all operate the same way, and at the same incredible low fare of 5 kopeks any distance, including transfers. It's the same fare for city buses, trolley-buses and streetcars. Public transport begins at about 6 a.m. and closes down by 1 a.m.

Ride the Metro

For the short-time visitor, the Metro system can seem rather daunting – especially in rush hours, and if you cannot read the Cyrillic alphabet. Some organised excursions incorporate a one-hour Moscow Metro circuit with their sightseeing tours, mainly to view the architecture and decor of individual stations. Certainly you should

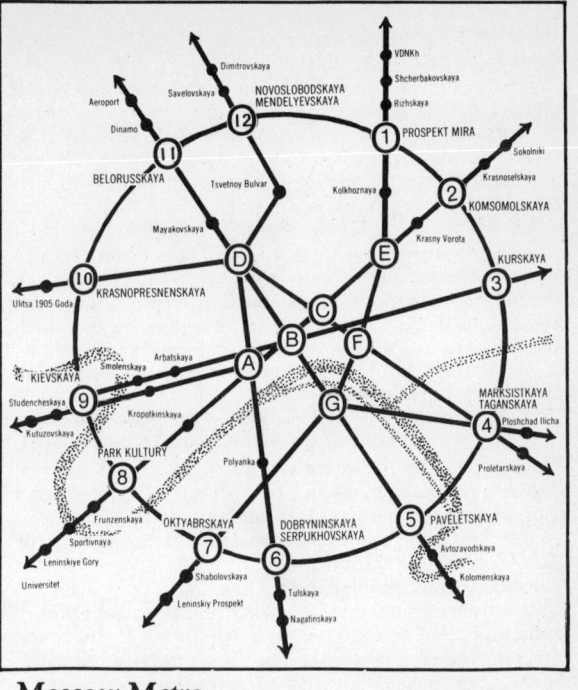

Moscow Metro
Central stations and the Circle Line

Stations on the Circle Line are located either on the Gardens Ring, or just outside it. On the Circle, there are 12 interchange stations – shown in capitals – connecting with the radial lines that go from Central Moscow to the suburbs.

The innermost stations are:

A – located by Lenin Library, corner of Kalinin Prospekt, facing entrance to Kremlin. Depending on which radial line, it will be described as Kalininskaya, Biblioteka Imeni Lenina, Arbatskaya, or Borovitskaya.

B – by entrance to Red Square, or Sverdlova Square. Depending on which radial line, it will be described as Prospekt Marksa, Ploshchad Revolyutsii, or Ploshchad Sverdlova.

C – Dzerzhinskaya.

D – by Pushkin Square. Described as Pushkinskaya, Chekhovskaya or Gorkovskaya.

E – Turgenevskaya and Kirovskaya.

F – Ploshchad Nogina.

G – Tretyakovskaya, or Novokuznetskaya.

take that introductory ride, if only to build confidence for using the Metro by yourself.

First you need a 5-kopek coin. Change machines can split a 10, 15 or 25-kopek piece. Deposit your 5-kopeks in the turnstile, and you're through. No tickets are issued.

The escalators are very deep, with neither ads nor graffiti to pass the time. You have to be nimble off the escalators, as they move really fast.

Which platform? Knowledge of the Cyrillic alphabet – or at least a smattering – is essential. If you haven't taken a crash course in Russian ABC, then before starting out you should get somebody in the hotel to write down your route in Russian. You can then ask the locals which platforms to use, and where to disembark. While waiting for your train, count how many stops to go before you reach your target station.

Notice the time clock at the end of the platform which ticks off the seconds since the previous train departed. During rush hours, there's only a 90-second interval between trains. Even outside those hours, you rarely wait more than three minutes for the next train. Mid-afternoon is best for travelling in less crowded conditions, and for sightseeing of the stations.

Journeys that require interchanges are more difficult. The connecting passages between one line and another demand skill in deciphering the destinations. If you're not careful, you can easily start going the wrong way round the Circle Line. Ask a Muscovite to point the way.

Buses, Trolley-buses and Trams

Trams are now phased out from Central Mocow, but buses and trolley-buses flourish. They are not easy to use by tourists who aren't around long enough to learn the routes. But if you're told the number to catch, why not give it a whirl?

You buy tickets in advance from 'kiock', 5 kopeks each to ride any distance. On entering the vehicle, watch how other travellers punch their ticket on an honours system. (Those who don't punch tickets probably have a season ticket.)

The same system applies in Leningrad, except that you can also board the vehicle at the front, and buy a single 5-kopek ticket from the driver. In Leningrad, trams still operate – in fact, it has the largest tram system in the world. For visitors they are probably simpler to use than the Metro.

Taxis

Taxis can be recognized by the letter 'T' in a chequered band, and they have meters. They may be difficult to find, and a problem to deal with. Best way to get a taxi is at a special stand, or through your hotel's Service Bureau.

Private car owners also operate as unofficial cabbies. This is quite acceptable, but first agree the fare. Otherwise, innocent tourists are scalped.

Sightseeing with Intourist

Most city sightseeing can be done by yourself, instead of through Intourist. But going it alone will cost you heavily on time. With Intourist, you get guide service, door-to-door transport and, above all, the facility of jumping the line.

On your own, you will need to speak at least Basic Russian; and you'll have to stand patiently in line with Soviet tourists, sometimes for a very long time to gain admission or buy a ticket. Many museums and galleries feature exhibits labelled only in Russian, and have no English-language catalogues.

Moscow-Leningrad, by Train

On the 400-mile inter-city train journey, you are recommended to take aboard some soft drinks and any snacks you may need for the journey. There is normally a buffet car, which gives waiter service for lunch. A typical 4-rouble lunch could feature a salad, soup, meat and potatoes or chicken and rice, and cake. It passes the time. Don't get off the train at stations en route, as often the halts are extremely brief. They don't whistle when the train's ready to go, so it's easy to be left behind!

The 7½-hour journey gives a good overview of Russian countryside: a landscape of pine trees, rivers, lakes and occasional villages with wooden houses that all have TV aerials sprouting alongside the chimneys.

1.6 Russian Sunday

Sunday in Moscow or Leningrad, shops and offices are closed, though food stores are open all day. Otherwise, there's plentiful choice of things to do. Without exception, every museum, gallery or exhibition is open. Intourist operates a full programme of city sightseeing tours and out-of-town excursions. Most interesting is to attend a religious service, especially if you are unfamiliar with the Russian Orthodox ritual.

Go Orthodox

There are 47 active Russian Orthodox churches in Moscow, and around 20 in Leningrad. In general, they hold daily services at 10 hrs, and at 17 or 18 hrs. On Sundays, there is an additional Mass at 7 hrs. Most visitors go for morning services as Vespers would clash with timing of the evening meal. The services are lengthy, and people come and go.

If you're staying at any of the central downtown hotels, such as the Rossiya, National, Metropole or Intourist, the nearest Orthodox church is St Nicholas on Nezhdanovoy Street. Take the third turning left up Gorky Street, go through a tall arch leading into Nezhdanovoy Street, and you can see the golden dome of the church built in 1629.

Attending a service is an emotional experience. Here is eternal Russia, which celebrated 1000 years of Christianity in 1988. You go in to the smell of incense, the sight of rich decoration and icons warmly lit by hundreds of candles, and the evocative sound of chanting by the bearded priests. A typical congregation is about 95% women, mostly grey-haired with a scattering of younger generation.

Services are crowded, with simultaneous worship in different areas of the church. The veneration of icons is an essential part of Orthodox ritual. A priest in a side-chapel gives a quiet sermon to a cluster of parishioners, undisturbed by the background chanting.

During a service you can respectfully move around, but obviously not take photographs. These self-supporting working churches are kept in beautiful condition by contributions from the faithful.

The experience is similar, whichever church you choose to attend. Near Cosmos Hotel, visit Our Lady of Tikhvin (Tikhvinskaya). From other hotels, check at the information desk for location of the nearest functioning church, and the exact times of services.

Likewise in Leningrad, ask directions from the hotel desk. The most memorable experience is to visit the Alexander Nevsky Lavra or Monastery, located immediately opposite Moscow Hotel. Lavra has services in its Cathedral of the Trinity on Monday to Friday at 10 hrs; and on Saturday and Sunday at 10, 11.30 and 13 hrs. Other working churches include St Nicholas Cathedral on Kommunarov Square; and Cathedral of the Transfiguration on Radishcheva Square (nearest Metro: Chernyshevskaya).

Other Services

In Moscow, the Jewish Synagogue is located at 8 Arkhipova Street, within walking distance of Rossiya Hotel (nearest Metro: Ploshchad Nogina). Daily services are held at 10 hrs, and at an hour before sunset. In Leningrad, the Synagogue is at 2 Lermontovskiy Prospekt (Bus 3, 27 or 43 to Theatre Square).

Roman Catholic services in Moscow are held at Church of St Louis, 12 Malaya Lubyanka Street (Metro: Dzerzhinsky Square). Daily mass at 8.30 and 10.30 hrs. In Leningrad: 7 Kovenskiy Pereulok (Metro: Ploshchad Vosstaniya).

Protestant services are held at the British and American embassies in Moscow – phone them for timings.

1.7 Shopping

Shops
In the USSR there are two types of shops.

1. Ordinary shops where Russians buy. Here, all prices are fixed in roubles, and payment is impossible in any other currency. There is no bargaining. In these shops, which always seem to be crowded, you must normally queue three times to complete a purchase: queue to choose what you want; queue at the cash desk to pay; queue again to collect your purchase. It's all rather a hassle, and takes time. If more than one article is wanted, collect up bills from the different counters, and then queue just once to pay. Most prices are high by Western standards. Choice is limited.

2. Beriozka shops, which do NOT accept payment in roubles, but only in foreign currency, travellers' cheques or leading Western credit cards. Prices are marked in roubles, and the cashier converts into any acceptable hard currency, such as sterling, dollars, D-Marks.

Some prices are slightly lower than in ordinary shops and the selection of goods is better. Beriozka stores (the word means Silver Birch Tree, a symbol of Siberia) are located mainly in hotels and airports. Most of the sales people speak English. The larger Beriozkas sell a complete range of tourist requirements from cigarettes and beverages – Coca-Cola to champagne – to furs, souvenirs and even Soviet automobiles such as the Volga or the Lada.

Good Buys
There are many Soviet products, arts and crafts which are worth buying. Here are some suggestions. Most of them are available in the Beriozka shops.

Matryoshka – very attractive wooden nesting dolls (unscrew the largest, and there's another nestling inside, and so down to thimble size). Made in Khotkova and Zagorsk, they cost £4 upwards, depending on size. For a connoisseur's private collection, a set of nine dolls, exquisitely painted, can cost over £2,000! There is also wide choice of costume dolls.

Palekh – Lacquered jewellery boxes and pill-boxes which make beautiful souvenirs, costing from about £40 – made by craftsmen descended from a long line of icon-painters.

Records and Cassettes – If you enjoy music, then it's worth buying classical albums or Soviet folk songs. Prices are extremely cheap, from £2.50 to £4 per record; £2 to £3 for cassettes. A complete opera on four records costs £8. Prices are the same in Russian rouble stores, and the choice even wider in the Melodiya shops of Moscow and Leningrad.

Balalaikas – These guitar-like musical instruments cost from about £9.

Watches, Optical & Photo Equipment – Good technology, at reasonable prices. Opera glasses at £8, for instance.

Furs – Luxury fur coats are beautiful, but expensive. At the other price extreme, treat yourself to a Russian rabbit-fur hat, fitted with ear-flaps that can be lowered beneath the chin in times of blizzard.

Caviar – rather expensive.

Vodka – A huge range of flavours, from lemon to pepper. Prices are around £8 a bottle – little different from UK price, and about the same for imported Scotch.

Other beverages – All Soviet wines are available. A bottle of pure fruit juice costs 50p, and the same for Coke or Pepsi.

Jewellery – Amber items are reasonable in price, but in silver settings rather than gold.

Books – Generally are cheap, compared with Western prices. There are well produced editions of art reproductions; English-language translations of Russian classics; and guide-books (though the English versions are often sold out).

Opening Hours – Russian Shops: 9-19 hrs (although times vary). Closed Sundays, except food shops.
Beriozkas: 10-14 & 15-19 hrs (until 18 hrs on Saturday).
Although most foreign visitors make the bulk of their purchases in the Beriozka stores, there is fascination in visiting the Russian shops, if only for sight of the typical Soviet life-style.

Queues are endemic to the system. When rumour spreads of worthwhile goodies at a particular counter, a line forms very rapidly. In their eagerness, many shoppers rush to join a queue and then – once they've secured a place – enquire what's being sold. In general, shops are full of *sensible* clothes, but customers are always looking for something more stylish.

In street underpasses, vendors erect a folding table and display the contents of a suitcase. An immediate crowd clusters round. Maybe it's books, or knitted hats, or plastic combs. Most visitors, before the end of their tour, get almost a Russian attitude of wanting to find out what's on offer, whenever they see a line-up.

It's also worth making the effort to find the nearest peasant market where private-sector products are sold – fruit, vegetables, meat, cottage cheese, honey, flowers. A typical covered market is State-owned. Individual farmers pay a small day-rental fee for a stall, and charge whatever the market will yield. The products are either surplus from what collectives must deliver to State stores at controlled prices; or are grown on 2½-acre plots which farmers cultivate for themselves.

Because of huge seasonal disparities between prices in the sunny southern republics and the north, many farmers find it economic to travel by air – possibly even 2,000 miles – to bring fruit or flowers for sale. The profit easily covers the modest airline fare. For instance, the fare from Baku to Leningrad is about 40 roubles, for a journey of 2,000 miles. It takes relatively few kilos of fruit to cover that cost.

1.8 Russian Cuisine

Hotel Meals

The standard Soviet hotel breakfast is substantial. A cold dish awaits you at the appointed hour – perhaps cheese, ham or other cold cuts. Then a hot dish arrives, such as omelette or boiled eggs. There is sliced white and rye bread, butter, jam and some kind of sweet bun. Coffee, if served, is usually in parsimonious quantity, carefully measured as one cup per person. But tea is available ad lib, Russian style without milk. It seems weak to the UK taste, unless you practise first at home with China tea. On request, milk is obtainable, but boiled. Most Brits end by accepting tea in Russian style. Others bring powdered milk from UK.

Lunches are usually four-course – a good hors d'oeuvre, soup, main course and dessert. Dinners are similar but three-course without the soup. Frequently the main course is meat and boiled potatoes with few green vegetables – though maybe with a tomato and cucumber salad. All-too-often, dessert is a slice of cake. Fruit seems rare. Gourmets consider that Russian cuisine is not among the world's greatest.

Most Soviet hotel catering managers have got the message that tourists don't want to spend hours on a meal. So groups normally have set menus, with no time-wasting between courses. Coloured soft drinks are usually included. But don't expect any ritual visitation by a wine waiter.

Instead, some express restaurants sell beer, Pepsi and Coke on a self-service basis as you enter.

Dining Out

If you wish to dine out, a reservation is virtually essential. Russians spread their meal through the whole evening, with dancing between courses. You must either get a firm reservation, or arrive very early (such as 5.30 p.m.). However you can easily book and pay for a meal through your tour representative. Eating out in the USSR can be expensive – like 25 roubles for a meal – but that includes wines and vodka. It's the price of a full evening, which can be quite memorable. Many co-operatives' restaurants have flourished since 1988, and you can now enjoy good food and music. Forget about fast service. You may think the waiters are moonlighting between courses. Just relax, and enjoy yourself Russian style, no clock-watching.

Here's a typical group meal served at the Georgian State restaurant called Aragvi, on Gorky Street in Moscow, at a cost of approximately 40 roubles per person. The meal started with a massive supply of bottles: vodka, blackberry juice, mineral water and white wine. The first wave of food comprised Satsni chicken with nuts and sauce; Lobio beans in sauce; and Lavash – delicious hot Georgian bread.

While the orchestra played Georgian folk-music, after a long pause came another surge of dishes: red cabbage in a red sauce; Sulguni hot cheese with cabbage, peppers and Kinza (which was supposed to be Georgian grasses, unless we got the translation wrong!). Then, after a suitable intermission, came young chicken shashlik, served with peppers, sauce and garlic. Meanwhile, the wines kept coming. Finally there was ice cream, which could certainly rival anything in the Western world for sheer flavour.

Some Soviet Specialities

During your stay, try some of the national dishes from at least one of the 15 Soviet Republics. Among the more widely known dishes are:

Caviar	– usually served on rye bread or with blini – delicious!
Borscht	– beetroot and cabbage soup
Solianka	– meat or fish soup flavoured with cucumber, tomatoes, olives, capers, lemon and sour cream
Beef Stroganoff	– the all time favourite!
Chicken Kiev	– Mouth-watering! Chicken with butter and garlic
Shashlik	– meat cooked on a skewer, similar to kebabs
Chanakhi	– a kind of stew

Fish	– sturgeon, herring, salmon and pike are the fish most usually found on menus
Pirogi	– pies filled with vegetables, meat, rice, poultry or fish
Blini	– the Russian form of pancake, sweet or savoury
Morozhenoye	– Russian ice cream. Superb! Sold from street stalls
Ramoraya Baba	– cake steeped in rum syrup

Beverages

Kvass	– a slightly alcoholic drink fermented from rye bread
Vodka	– the best known brand is Stolichnaya. Vodka is served by weight, and drunk neat from small glasses in a single gulp
Water	– You are recommended to drink bottled mineral water, not tap water. But tap water is quite safe for washing and for cleaning teeth.

Eating Out During the Daytime

If you're on half board, where should you eat midday? Apart from your hotel which will have at least one dining room or well stocked buffet, you may have difficulty in finding outside restaurants – particularly if you don't want to queue. But for a quick snack or refreshment, there are plentiful stand-up cafeterias. Explain what you want in your fluent Russian, pay first at the cash desk, and you're in business. Sample prices: glass of tea 10 kopeks; coffee 40 kopeks.

Easiest is to buy from sidewalk stalls that sell cakes, sausages, hot meat pies, salami or cheese on a slice of bread, soft drinks and ice cream. Typical are the barbecue stands, which offer grilled kebabs at 2 roubles for 100 grammes. Each portion is separately weighed and costed. The flavour can be excellent. Worth trying, for the fun of it.

1.9 Nightlife

Evening meals in Moscow and Leningrad are normally taken early – 6 p.m. is fairly standard – with express service that shuttles through in a brisk 45 minutes. That's in contrast to Russian-style 'dining out', when the dinner, wines and dancing are spread across three hours or more.

To make the most of your trip, try different entertainment each evening: opera, ballet, circus, folklore show and a full Russian dinner out at a restaurant. Don't miss any of them, even if they're not normally your scene! If you still have a spare evening, why not go to a symphony concert?

Theatre

Opera and ballet tickets are not so much sold, as allocated. First call goes to people and groups on the inside track, including diplomats and visiting delegations. Next in line comes Intourist, ordering for visitors who are paying in foreign currency. Lowest priority are the local citizens who queue patiently at ticket windows, and hope that finally they'll strike lucky for that cherished seat at the Kirov or the Bolshoi.

The rouble price on the ticket may be substantially less than you are paying Intourist. It's not a rip-off. The Soviet justification is that the price for Russians is heavily subsidized. The hard currency cost for foreign visitors is closer to the world market level for a theatre performance of similar international class. If transport is included, your tour representative will get you to the show on time.

If you're unfamiliar with the opera, try to find someone who knows the story. The programmes on sale are all in Russian, even though foreign tourists make up a high proportion of the audience.

Folk Groups

Soviet folk-dance groups provide a superb evening's entertainment. The companies that give theatre performances are of highly professional international standard. A typical group consists of over a hundred performers: fifty singers, a dozen musicians and forty dancers. The pace and vivacity of the shows, and the colourful costumes, make up a brilliant show. Superb!

Circus

The circus is a permanent feature of every major Soviet city. It provides good traditional entertainment of universal appeal: acrobats, trapeze artistes, clowns and comedy dog and monkey acts. There's much less emphasis on the old-time caged animal performances. Wildly exciting are the displays of Cossack, Armenian or Kazak horsemanship. Unforgettable!

Nightclubs

In Russia, nightlife is dead by 11 p.m. There are no nightclubs. The only place for a nightcap is in currency bars of the larger hotels which sometimes present a cabaret or folk dancing.

1.10 *Learn Russian ABC*

As a basic minimum, at least spend a little time in decoding the Russian alphabet. It will greatly add to your holiday pleasure, helping you to read a word here and there, or to recognise a street name.

Start with what's familiar. These six letters are the same in Russian and English: A, E, K, M, O, T. The only slightly tricky letter is 'E', which is pronounced 'ye' as in English 'yes'. If there are two dots over the E – Ë – then it becomes 'yo' as in 'yonder'.

Then we have another group of six letters which are printed the same, but are pronounced differently:

B – pronounced like English V
H – pronounced like English N
P – pronounced like English R
C – pronounced like English S
Y – pronounced like English OO
X – pronounced as in Scottish 'loch'

Then there's a reminder that the Russian Cyrillic alphabet was a revamp of Greek. So, if you can remember some of those symbols used in mathematics or physics – or if you have picked up any of the letters from a Greek holiday – here's another batch that can easily be remembered:

Γ – gamma, which equals G
Δ – delta, which equals D
Λ – lamda which equals L
Π – pi, which equals P
Φ – fee, which equals F

Now we come to the hard core, which seems more baffling. Three of them look like familiar letters, written backwards:

Я – looks like backwards R, but is equal to YA, as in **yarn**
И – looks like backwards N, but is equal to I, as in machine.
Й – like backwards N with an accent – equals consonant Y.

Two more letters are easily confused:

З – like a figure 3, but it's letter Z as in zoo
Э – like a backward-written E, and it really is E as in net.

The ordeal by Russian ABC is almost ended. There's a group of four which sound like a steam train when you pronounce them in alphabetical sequence:

Ц – ts – as in pits or **Ts**ar
Ч – ch – as in **ch**arm
Ш – sh – as in **sh**ip
Щ – shch – as in Kru**shch**ev

Then there are two decorative letters:

Ж – a ZH sound, like French **je** or the central sound of mea**s**ure. Ladies should learn this one, which indicates which WC door is theirs. (Men should head for 'M').
Ю – a U sound, as in **u**nity.

Finally, a few bits and bobs, all looking like variations of the English lower-case 'b'. Two of them you can just ignore – Ъ and Ь . They are respectively 'hard' and 'soft' signs which contribute nothing to your understanding of Russian ABC. Then Ы is equal to our letter 'I', as in d**i**g. Lastly there's Б which is our very own 'B' as in **B**olshevik.

It's worth the few minutes' headache to crack the system. To give you practice, here's a short word-list:

да	*da*	yes
нет	*nyet*	no
бар	*bar*	bar
буфет	*bufyet*	buffet
ресторан	*restoran*	restaurant
кафе	*kafe*	café
лифт	*lift*	lift
телефон	*telefon*	telephone
магазин	*magazeen*	shop
Гум	*Goom*	GUM (department store)
фунты	*funti*	pounds
доллары	*dollari*	dollars
чеки	*cheki*	cheques
такси	*taksi*	taxi
стой	*stoy*	stop
Ленин	*Lenin*	Lenin
музей	*muzey*	Museum
площадь	*ploshchad*	Square
проспект	*Prospekt*	Avenue
улица	*ulitsa*	Street
мужчин	*moozhcheen*	men
женщин	*zhenshchin*	ladies

Chapter Two

2.1 Welcome to Moscow

Located on important trade routes in the heart of the Russian plain, Moscow has been at the focal point of history since the original Kremlin – walled castle – was built over eight centuries ago. Often, that history has been supremely uncomfortable. In 1237, Moscow was sacked by the Mongols, who controlled Russia with their Tatar allies until 1480. But by mid-16th century – when Ivan the Terrible was crowned as the first Tsar – Moscow had become one of Europe's largest cities, though it still suffered from Tatar capture in 1571 when most of the city was burned.

During Ivan's reign, Moscow opened up much more to the West. English merchants settled near the Kremlin walls in the 1550's. The city's status continued to grow during the rule of Boris Godunov. After his death in 1605 there came seven turbulent years of civil wars, rebellions, and invasions from Poland and Sweden. Peace returned in 1613 with a Romanov elected as Tsar – first of the dynasty, who ruled for over 300 years until their final abdication in March 1917.

During the earlier centuries, virtually all dwellings were timber-built. Hence, when Napoleon marched in to Moscow in 1812, the city again caught fire, probably through carelessness. Over 80 per cent of houses were destroyed. But within a few years Moscow was rebuilt, with a larger population than before.

Since the Revolution, most of that 19th-century Moscow – except for the historic core – has undergone major surgery: main boulevards greatly widened, slum dwellings replaced by modern apartment blocks, new public buildings established.

With the continued extension of the Metro system, many new residential neighbourhoods have been developed to accommodate Moscow's ever growing population (now 8,800,000). Essentially the Moscow of today is a modern city, built on a grand scale, though the austerity of the 20th-century architecture has been softened by gardens and parks. One third of Moscow is green space.

Red Square and the Kremlin are the greatest tourist

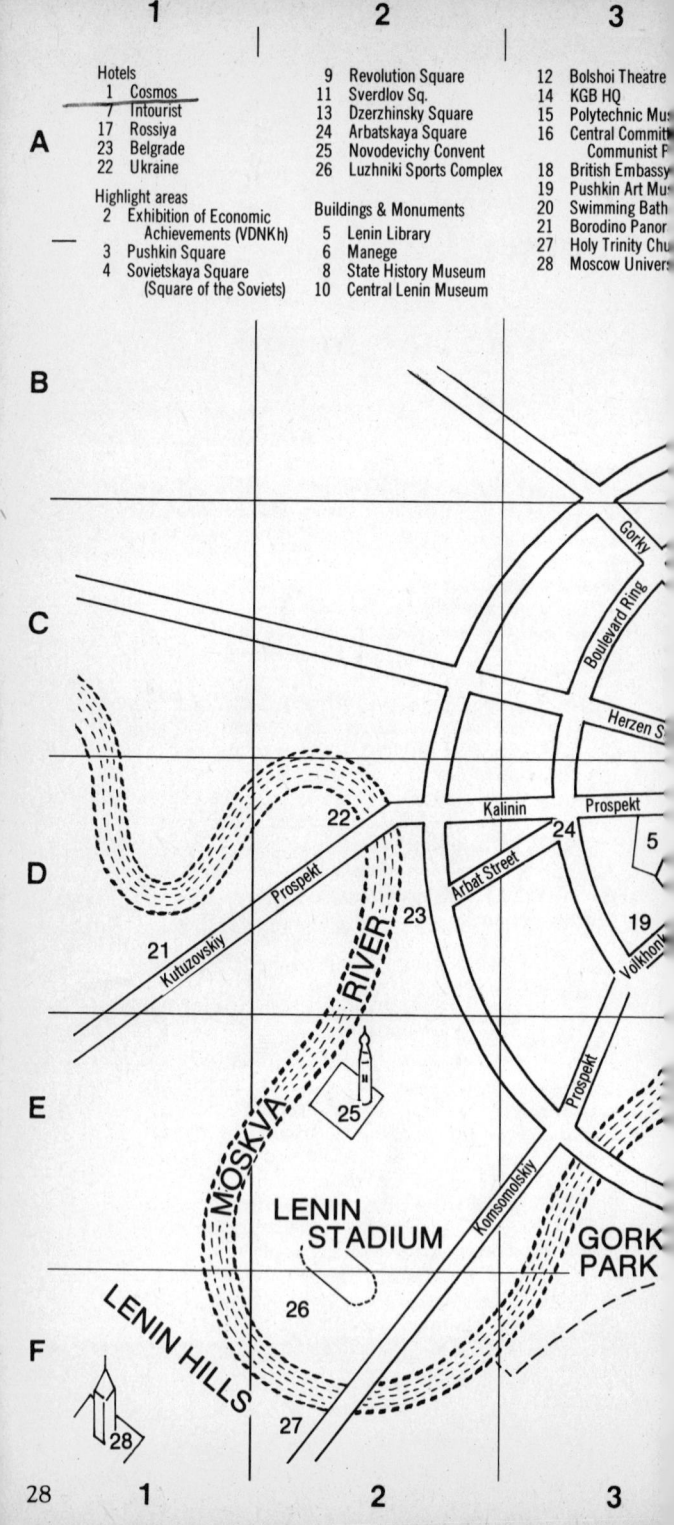

	1	**2**	**3**

Hotels
1 Cosmos
7 Intourist
17 Rossiya
23 Belgrade
22 Ukraine

Highlight areas
2 Exhibition of Economic
   Achievements (VDNKh)
3 Pushkin Square
4 Sovietskaya Square
   (Square of the Soviets)

9 Revolution Square
11 Sverdlov Sq.
13 Dzerzhinsky Square
24 Arbatskaya Square
25 Novodevichy Convent
26 Luzhniki Sports Complex

Buildings & Monuments
5 Lenin Library
6 Manege
8 State History Museum
10 Central Lenin Museum

12 Bolshoi Theatre
14 KGB HQ
15 Polytechnic Mus
16 Central Committ
   Communist F
18 British Embassy
19 Pushkin Art Mus
20 Swimming Bath
21 Borodino Panor
27 Holy Trinity Chu
28 Moscow Univers

28

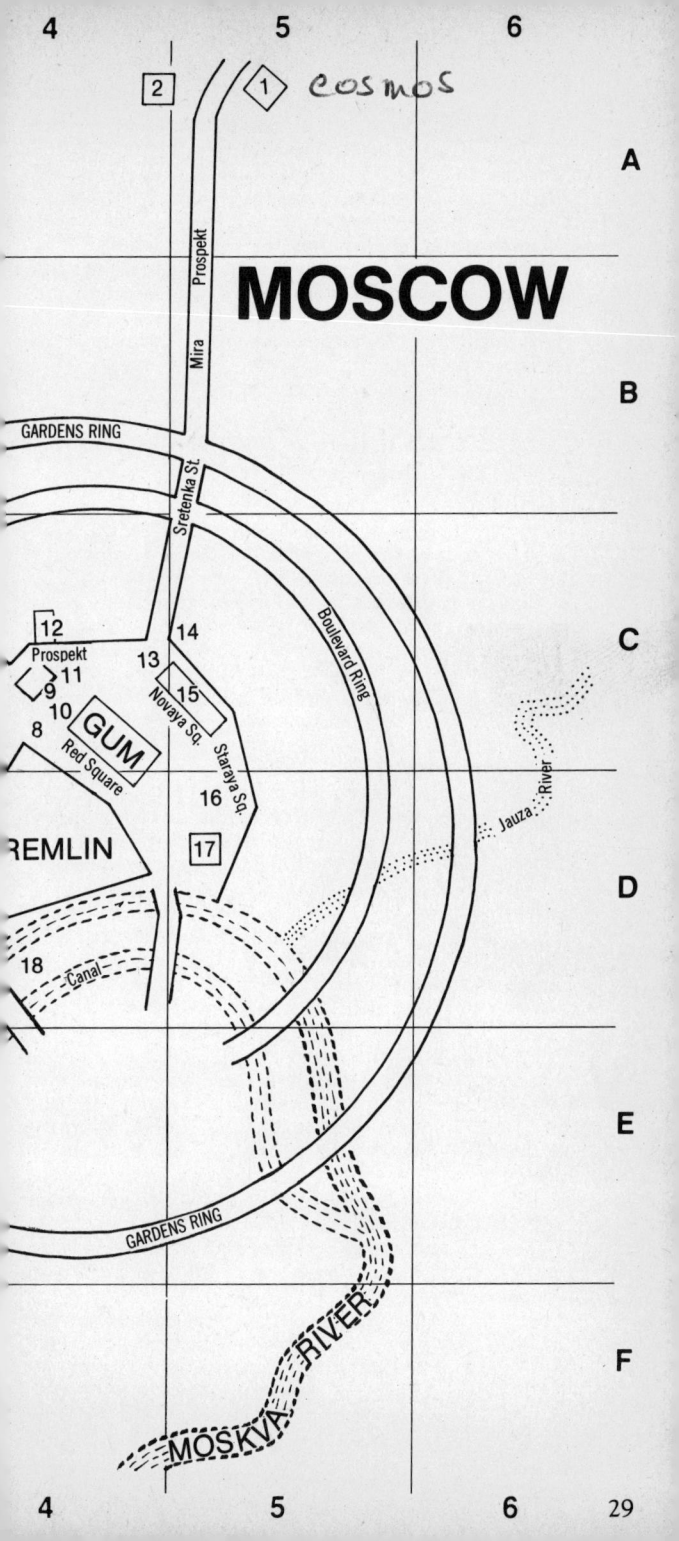

attractions – for Soviet people and foreign visitors alike. Watching the changing of the guard at Lenin's Mausoleum there'll be Europeans and Americans, Japanese, sari-clad Indians and Georgians, Armenians and Azerbaijanis. Moscow is the great magnet.

There's never enough time to see everything. Most visitors are on the go, every day, with city sightseeings and excursions, museums, galleries and evening entertainment. The potential is enormous. The only solution is to pick out the highlights which interest you most – and resolve to stay longer next time!

2.2 Find Your Way Around Moscow

The city layout is a cartwheel. The hub, dead centre, is the triangular-shaped Kremlin, with Red Square outside the eastern wall. West and south, the inner city is bounded by the Moskva River, twisting like a demented snake, while the tributary Jauza River forms an eastern boundary.

Enclosing that inner hub is a semi-circle of major squares, linked principally by Marx Prospekt and New and Old Squares – Novaya Ploshchad and Staraya Ploshchad – with the rivers to complete the enclosure. Principal public buildings are located around these squares – all within a few minutes' walk of Red Square.

About a mile further out is the Boulevard Ring with long strips of parks and greenery running down the central reservation, forming a dual carriageway. Along the 6-mile Boulevard Ring are many cherished 18th-century mansions, well preserved.

Another mile further out is the precise circle called the Gardens Ring. This marked the original city limits, with ramparts until the 18th century. Much of the Garden Ring today is 14 traffic lanes wide. The 10-mile Garden Ring is divided into 17 sectors, each with its own name. Virtually everything of interest to visitors is contained within that circle, or just outside.

Fanning out from the inner hub are major radial highways. The most important are those which lead westwards or north. Kalinin Prospekt continues as the Mozhaisk Highway – the M1 Motorway to Western Europe via Minsk, Brest, Warsaw and Berlin. Gorky Street finally becomes the M10 Motorway to Leningrad.

In the segments formed by these radial highways, many of the lanes and streets retain something of their 19th-century atmosphere. A casual stroll in these side-streets can be rewarding.

Even further beyond the Garden Ring is an outer ring-road which forms almost a complete beltway around Moscow. Making Londoners feel at home, part of the

ring-road is the M25 – signposted in white on a blue
background – but no traffic jams.

Metro

Moscow's superb Metro system parallels the city's
highway layout. Radial lines fan out from the central
squares along Marx Prospekt. These are linked mainly by
the Circle Line, which follows closely to the Gardens Ring,
or just outside.

2.3   Red Square

There's an excitement about standing in the world's most
famous square. Fifteen acres of cobble-stones, spread out
beneath the Kremlin walls, Red Square is one of the great
focal-points of history. You've seen it all before, dozens of
times in newspapers, magazines and on TV: setting for the
big Soviet parades on May 1 and November 7.

Go back five hundred years, and this area was laid out as
a market place, with rows of artisan and trader stalls. A
moat separated the 'Big Market' (as the square was
originally called) from the Kremlin wall. In the 17th
century, as fine buildings surrounded the market place, it
became known as 'Red' Square – *krasnaya*, which in old
Russian meant 'beautiful'. Today's name has nothing to
do with political colouring. It was Red Square, even in
Tsarist times.

In fact, red is the dominant colouring – red-brick walls
of the Kremlin and of the Historical Museum; illuminated
red stars a-top the Kremlin towers; red granite for Lenin's
tomb; red banners for slogans, when the Square is being
prepared for parades. On big occasions, up to two million
people have squeezed into the Square.

To the Soviet people, a visit to Red Square – and
especially to the Lenin Mausoleum – is like a pilgrimage.
No smoking is allowed. Apart from official limousines
that speed through the Spasskaya Gate into the Kremlin,
Red Square is a pedestrian precinct. The last person who
landed there in a private aircraft was prosecuted as a
hooligan.

Lenin Mausoleum

Below the Kremlin wall is the Lenin Mausoleum, built of
red granite with a symbolic mourning band of black
iridescent mineral rock called labradorite. It is very
simple, and deeply impressive. Daily except Mondays and
Fridays, a long queue forms, sometimes lasting hours, to
gain admittance to the air-conditioned vault where Lenin's
body is embalmed. Intourist groups file through at lunch
time, with less queuing.

Afterwards, visitors pass behind the Mausoleum. Along

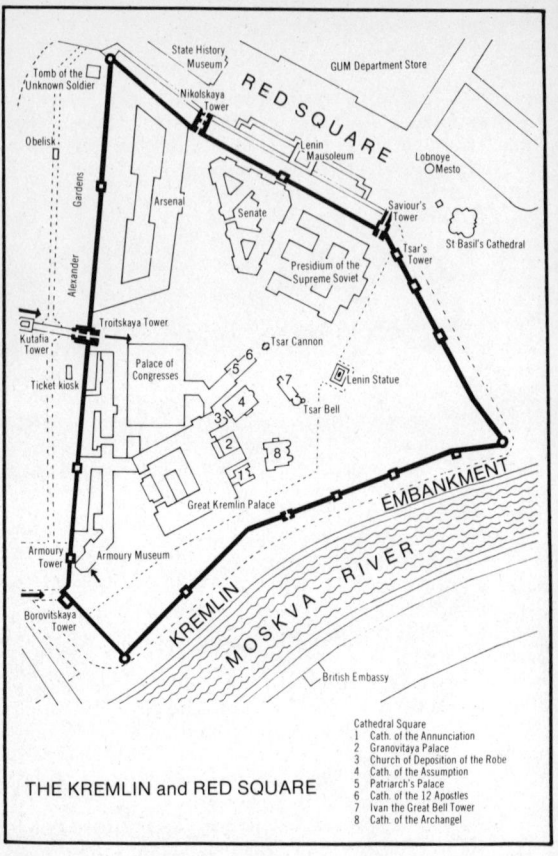

THE KREMLIN and RED SQUARE

Cathedral Square
1 Cath. of the Annunciation
2 Granovitaya Palace
3 Church of Deposition of the Robe
4 Cath. of the Assumption
5 Patriarch's Palace
6 Cath. of the 12 Apostles
7 Ivan the Great Bell Tower
8 Cath. of the Archangel

the Kremlin wall between the Nikolskaya and Spasskaya Towers are memorial tablets and tombstones to Soviet politicians and a select band of foreign revolutionaries: the ultimate honour, like being buried in Westminster Abbey. Among those who rate a slot in the Kremlin wall are General Zhukov (of World War II fame), and Yury Gagarin (the first man in space).

The Mausoleum doubles as the reviewing stand from where Soviet leaders watch the big parades which come marching down Gorky Street, into Red Square. On either side of the Mausoleum are tribunes of honour for ten thousand VIPs and distinguished guests.

Just before every hour, a three-soldier guard goose-steps out from the Spasskaya Gate to the Lenin Mausoleum. With split-second timing, the soldiers complete the guard-changing ceremony precisely as the hour strikes.

St Basil's Cathedral

The most eye-catching sight in Red Square is St Basil's Cathedral, virtually a symbol of Russia. Its nine rainbow-coloured onion and pineapple-shaped domes look like hot-air balloons ready to take off.

This folk-art church was built in 1555–1560, on the order of Ivan the Terrible, to celebrate the conquest in 1552 of Kazan, the last stronghold of the Tatars. Ivan's victory took place on October 1st, the Festival of the Intercession; so the church was originally called the Intercession Cathedral. A few years later, the remains of the Holy Fool Basil the Blessed were moved to the Cathedral, which then more popularly became known as St Basil's.

In 1812, French troops plundered the Cathedral, and stabled their horses there. Napoleon gave orders for St Basil's to be blown up, but fortunately the command was not carried out.

Today, the church is the most-photographed monument in the Soviet Union. Nobody with a camera can resist that bizarre fairy-tale fantasy. Night-time floodlights make the peppermint-rock colours stand out even more sharply than by day. The church is open daily except Tuesday, and is preserved as a branch of the Historical Museum located at the other end of the Square. Inside, each dome is a separate chapel.

Away left behind St Basil's stands the 12-storey Rossiya Hotel – one of the world's largest, accommodating 5,300 guests. Built 1971, the Rossiya also includes the 3,000-capacity Central Concert Hall, a very large Beriozka shop, and a cinema.

Lobnoye Mesto

Between St Basil's and the GUM Department Store is a circular stone structure with steps, enclosed by wrought-iron gates: Lobnoye Mesto (The Place of Skulls). From this platform, state decrees of the Tsars were proclaimed. It was also a grim place of public execution, where Ivan the Terrible set the tone on how to deal with dissent. Stenka Razin, leader of a peasant revolt in 1670, died here. In 1698, Peter the Great started heads rolling for 2,000 executions.

Saviour's Tower (Spasskaya Tower)

For the Soviet people, St Saviour's Tower – Spasskaya Tower – is like Big Ben for the British, with a big clock and a carillon. The Kremlin Chimes are broadcast as a regular time-check over Radio Moscow. The original installation was made in 1625 by an Englishman named Christopher Holloway.

The tower was considered sacred, with an icon of Christ over the entrance. All visitors had to doff their hats while crossing through the gateway. One person refused – Napoleon, in 1812. But as he crossed the gateway, a gust of wind blew off his hat: perhaps a harbinger of the Retreat from Moscow – an omen that the elements were on Russia's side!

The Spasskaya Gate was built by an Italian architect in 1491. The gothic tower was added in 17th century, and topped by a two-headed Romanov eagle. The eagle was replaced in 1937 with a red star, to mark the 20th year of the Revolution.

This is the VIP entrance to the Kremlin. Admission for the general public is through two gateways on the west side of the Kremlin, from Alexander Gardens.

The Kremlin Walls

Next to Saviour's Tower – left – is Tsar's Tower, located where Ivan the Terrible enjoyed a good view of the executions. At the top end of Red Square is St Nicholas Tower, restored in 1816 after being destroyed by the French. In 1917 this Gate was stormed by Bolshevik soldiers who captured the Kremlin.

The red flag above the Kremlin walls never droops. It is kept permanently fluttering by an air-stream that puffs out from the flagpole.

GUM Department Store

Directly across Red Square, facing the Lenin Mausoleum, is GUM department store. GUM (pronounced 'Goom') stands for the Russian initials of State Universal Store. Originally the site was an open air market comprising hundreds of stalls, in long trading rows. Today's building was erected in 1888: like an immense greenhouse, a shopping mall with three streets of shops on two floors. Entrances are at each end of the building – not on Red Square itself. (See the 'Shopping' section for a recommended visit to GUM).

State History Museum

Another 19th-century building is the red-brick State History Museum, at the northern end of Red Square. It focuses on the long history of the peoples inhabiting the Soviet Union, from Stone Age till the late 19th century. Of special interest are clothes and possessions of Ivan the Terrible; and Napoleon's bed which was abandoned during the 1812 retreat from Moscow.

The museum is open Monday and Thursday-Saturday 10.30-17.30 hrs; Wednesday and Sunday 12-19 hrs. Closed Tuesday.

Alexander Gardens

Walk out of Red Square between the Kremlin Wall and the History Museum. Turn left at the corner, and you enter Alexander Gardens. Lime trees grow in what formerly was part of the Kremlin moat. The Gardens are especially pretty in May, when springtime tulips are in full bloom.

At the corner of the Kremlin wall is the Tomb of the Unknown soldier, marked by an eternal flame. Visitors queue to pay homage. Especially touching is the custom that newlyweds come here to lay a bouquet – first stop after their wedding ceremony. Particularly on Saturdays, bridal cars are lined up twenty or thirty at a time. The Soviet Union's appalling wartime losses – twenty million dead – are not forgotten. Along the path, memorial stones commemorate cities which were major battlefields.

Next is the Obelisk to Revolutionary Thinkers, which originally was erected to mark three centuries of Romanov rule. Names of Tsars were swapped for pioneers of revolutionary thought: obviously Marx and Engels, but also including Sir Thomas More (16th-century author of *Utopia*).

Further along, Alexander Gardens is crossed by a white bridge. That is the main public entrance into the Kremlin – from Kutafia Tower by the roadside where tour coaches disembark, through Trinity (Troitskaya) Tower. An alternative gateway is at the furthest end of Alexander Gardens, through Borovitsky Tower – the most direct approach to the State Armoury.

2.4 Inside the Kremlin

During the Stalin era, the Kremlin grounds were kept tightly shut, aloof and forbidding. But since 1955 the Kremlin has been wide open to visitors from 10 a.m. till 7 p.m. every day, entrance free. Just walk in, through either the Trinity Tower or the Borovitskaya Gate. It is best to take a half-day guided tour, with the advantage of a knowledgeable guide and a scheduled time-slot for Intourist entrance to the fabulous Armoury treasure-house. There is also evening admittance through Trinity Tower for those attending concert or theatre performances at the Palace of Congresses.

Kremlin is a Russian word for fortress or citadel. According to the first historic mention of Moscow, Prince Yuri Dolgoruky (the Long-Armed) met his ally and relative Prince Sviatoslav here in 1147. They decided to built a fortress on this hillside at the confluence of the Moskva and Neglinnaya Rivers, where the site was protected on three sides by the rivers.

There were many fortresses called Kremlin, in other Russian towns. But Moscow's Kremlin acquired special importance, as the centre of resistance against the Mongol and Tatar hordes. The geographical location was ideal, at the crossing of trade routes.

Destroyed several times during its early history, the Kremlin took its present shape and appearance from 1485 onwards, when Italian architects – renowned for their know-how as fortification engineers – were invited to Moscow. They designed the existing layout of the 67-acre triangular site, with 1.4 miles of massive walls that rise up to 60 feet high.

Palace of Congresses

On the right as you enter the Kremlin grounds from Trinity Tower, the long building of glass, steel and white marble is the Palace of Congresses. More than half the building is below ground, to avoid spoiling the historic Kremlin skyline. Opened in 1961, the 6,000-seat auditorium is the main conference hall for Party rallies. You've probably seen it on TV, when Mikhail Gorbachev makes one of his big speeches.

It doubles as a mammoth theatre for Bolshoi opera and ballet performances, film festivals, New Year gala events and the like. Acoustics are superb, and there are no columns to block your view of the enormous stage. During intervals, theatre-goers whizz up on high-speed escalators to the top-floor buffet for sandwiches, canapés and a bird's-eye view of the floodlit golden domes of the Kremlin cathedrals. What more could you want for your money?

The Senate

Continue past the Palace of Congresses, keeping inside the white lines. Police make despairing efforts, trilling with whistles and wagging their fingers in warning, to keep tourists off the broad cobbled roadway. Occasional black limousines swish past. Across that parade-ground expanse are working buildings for the administration of Soviet affairs.

The V-shaped yellow and white building, with flag flying over a green dome, is the Senate – the seat of government, where all the big Kremlin decisions are made. On the third floor, Lenin had his office and private apartment, still preserved. There's no admission for ordinary mortals, but you can console yourself by seeing a detailed replica in the Lenin Museum. On the floor below, the USSR Council of Ministers hold their cabinet meetings.

Tsar's Cannon

A fascinated crowd is always gathered around the next point of interest: the massive 40-ton Tsar Cannon. It was cast in 1586 to frighten enemies of Tsar Fyodor, the simple-minded son of Ivan the Terrible. Fortunately for the gunners, the cannon never fired any of its one-ton balls which measured three feet in diameter. Several of them are stacked ready, beside the cannon.

Tsar's Bell and Ivan the Great Bell-Tower

Towering above the Kremlin, the Bell-Tower with two golden domes has 21 bells, the largest weighing 66 tons. Built in the 16th century, the belfry originally served as a strategic watchtower.

On a stone pedestal next to the Bell-Tower stands the world's largest bell – the Tsar Kolokol, which weighs over 200 tons. Like the Tsar's Cannon which never fired, the Tsar's Bell has never pealed. Nobody could solve the problem of how to raise it into the belfry. After a fire, a chunk of the Bell fell off. Altogether, it's quite useless. But it's a great tourist attraction.

Kremlin Gardens

For a few minutes, ignore the Cathedral Square to the right, but continue across the cobbled square to a statue of Lenin, and a pleasant little park with fir trees and flowers. You're then far enough back to take pictures of the Bell Tower. From the gardens you also get good views over the Moskva River, and the southern line of Kremlin walls and towers.

Cathedral Square

Cathedral Square is the most central point of the Kremlin, surrounded by five churches and Ivan the Great Bell-Tower – all preserved in immaculate condition. Here is picture-book Russia: a tiny area which has been the setting of innumerable historical events over the past 800 years. When the sun sparkles on the golden cupolas, it's a fairytale sight. Notice the triumphant crosses above recumbent crescents, symbolizing the victory of Christianity over Islam.

Each of the churches had its specialized function in the life-style of Russian royalty. Clockwise around the Square, the Tsars were christened and wed in the Cathedral of the Annunciation; crowned in Assumption; buried in Archangel Michael, with portrait worked into the mural of the Last Judgement.

Some of the churches may be closed during your visit. Restoration and upkeep is a constant, on-going process, and has continued steadily since the 1920's. The churches are non-functioning, but are cherished as museums, part of the Russian heritage. Entrance tickets are sold at a kiosk in Alexander Gardens, below the bridge into Trinity Tower.

Cathedral of the Annunciation

Facing Archangel Michael Cathedral across the square is the golden-domed Cathedral of the Annunciation. The six gilded cupolas were erected after an original three were damaged by fire in 1562. The Cathedral was used as the private chapel of the Tsars, particularly for weddings and christenings. It houses fascinating icons and paintings of the 13th to 16th centuries – some attributed to Andrei Rublev (greatest of the Russian icon painters) and Theophanes the Greek. The monument is like a superb art gallery.

Cathedral of the Assumption (or Dormition)

Pride of place goes to the five-domed Cathedral of the Assumption, built in 1479 by an architect from Bologna. His brief was to pattern the building on the 12th century cathedral of the same name in the city of Vladimir. This marriage of Russian and Italian styles produced a masterpiece. It became Russia's most important church – setting for all the big ceremonial occasions, including the crowning of Tsars and Emperors.

Decoration of the church – icons, murals, woodcarving – occupied Russia's finest artists and craftsmen for centuries. The sheer volume of art-work is almost overpowering. Most visitors rest content with the overall impression, and skip the details. Of special interest is a beautifully-carved wooden throne purpose-built for Ivan the Terrible.

In 1812, Napoleon's troops used the church as a stable, and bolted with five tons of silver and 600 pounds of gold. The Cossacks liberated the silver, and presented the Cathedral with the half-ton silver chandelier which now dangles from the dome. Shaped like a sheaf of wheat, the chandelier is called *Harvest*.

Church of the 12 Apostles and the Patriarch's Palace

Built in 1655–56, the church once served as the Patriarch's private place of worship. Since 1963 the Patriarch's Palace has housed the Museum of 17th century Applied Art and Everyday Life.

Cathedral of Archangel Michael

Built by an Italian at the beginning of the 16th century – 1505 to 1508 – the Cathedral of Archangel Michael combines Russian style with a touch of Italy. It replaced an earlier church dating from 1333. The site was the main burial vault of the Tsars and Grand Princes of Moscow from 14th to 18th centuries. Ivan the Terrible is buried behind the iconostasis, with his elder son (whom he killed) close by.

Church of the Deposition of the Robe

Opened to the public in 1965 after being restored to its original 15th century glory, this church contains brilliant frescoes and icons from the 17th century. Showcases display rare carvings from the 15th to 18th centuries.

Great Kremlin Palace

Peter the Great transferred the capital of Russia to St Petersburg in 1712. But Moscow never lost its importance as a political and religious centre. Russian Emperors and Empresses returned here for coronation and wedding ceremonies, to pay tribute to their ancestors, and to worship at the shrines. Their Moscow town house was the Great Kremlin Palace, which was frequently altered during the 18th century. Its present appearance, with the long yellow and white facade, dates from a major re-build in 1838-49.

When Moscow became the capital again in 1918, the Palace became the meeting place for the Supreme Soviet of the USSR and of the Russian Federation. It's still used for these State events, but the general public can only admire the building from outside.

The Armoury

Down the hill past the Great Kremlin Palace, towards the Borovitskaya Tower, and there's the modest entry to the Armoury Palace. Toilets to the left, cloakrooms to the right – and then continue through and up the stairs to one of the world's great hoards of Imperial treasure.

These art riches were amassed by the Grand Princes and Tsars of Russia over the centuries – combination of diplomatic gifts, purchase, and special manufacture in the Kremlin's own workshops. The workshops covered a broad range of skills: production of medieval weapons and armour, dress harness for royal horses, textiles for royal bedding and clothing, silver and gold objects of every description.

The present Armoury Palace was purpose-built in early 19th century to house the collection. The museum layout is superb, with information in English. There are nine rooms – numbers 1 to 5 on the top floor; 6 to 9 below.

Room 1 – Devoted to Russian gold and silver articles, 12th to 16th century. It shows development of Russian jewellers' art, particularly of gold and silverware made in Moscow from the end of the 14th century; and 16th century articles made in the Kremlin workshops.

Room 2 – Russian gold, silver and jewellery from 17th to early 20th century, including exquisite 18th-century snuff boxes. To see incredible workmanship, make sure you find the case displaying the Fabergé creations.

Fabergé was the greatest of the 19th-century Russian jewellers. The firm was founded 1842 in St Petersburg, and it finally employed 500 staff. As the most successful jeweller of the age, Fabergé produced all kinds of ornamental objects of gold and precious stones, silverware, snuff boxes and cigarette cases. World-famous were his surprise Easter eggs, which were a triumph of miniaturization.

Room 3 – Oriental and Western European Gala Arms and Armour, 15th to 19th century. Especially rich in Oriental weapons made by Iranian and Turkish craftsmen in 16th and 17th centuries. The early guns, shields, scabbards, helmets and swords are examples more of the jewellers' art, than the armaments manufacturer. Battle-axes and maces are encrusted end to end with precious stones.

Room 4 – Russian arms and armour, mostly 12th to early 19th century battledress, ceremonial swords and parade sabres. Many items belonged to famous statesmen and military men.

Room 5 – West European silver, 13th to 19th centuries. This is claimed to be the world's largest collection of European silver, mostly brought to Moscow by ambassadors and merchants as diplomatic offerings. If the gifts were considered worthy, they went into the Tsar's treasury.

Look specially for the unique collection of massive English silverware from Tudor and Stuart times. The keyword is massive. A brimming tankard would need real muscle-power for a drinking session.

Room 6 – Precious fabrics, pictorial and decorative embroidery, and lay clothes in Russia 16th to early 20th century.

Room 7 – State ceremonial regalia from 13th to 18th centuries – coronets, sceptres and orbs, crosses, chains and necklets. Some items were symbols of State power – the Cap of Monomachus, for instance, heavy with jewels and rimmed with fur, used in coronation ceremonies.

Also on show is a range of royal thrones, all somewhat lacking in comfort. A throne studded with several thousand diamonds has to be rock-hard. The oldest throne, faced with carved ivory, was Ivan the Terrible's.

Room 8 – A great collection of formal dress worn in 16th to 18th centuries by horses in royal service: saddles and stirrups, horse-cloths, headbands and pieces. Many items were gifts brought by ambassadors from Iran, Turkey, Poland and Germany.

Room 9 – 16th to 18th century State carriages, made by craftsmen from all over Europe. You could spend an hour in this room alone, studying the design, decoration and furnishings of these vintage vehicles. The oldest model was sent to Boris Godunov by King James 1. Note the styling changes from late Renaissance to Baroque, Classical, Regency and Rococo.

In 1742, Empress Elizabeth I rode to her coronation from St Petersburg to Moscow in a 23 h.p. sleigh that was more like a mobile home, with table, chairs, divan and charcoal-fired central heating.

2.5 The Rest of Basic Moscow

If you're a first-time visitor, exploring Moscow on your own is not easy. Unless you know the alphabet, it's difficult to read street names. It takes a while to get orientated and learn the transport system. A sightseeing tour can be arranged by your tour representative. This will cover the main points of interest.

The guides do a thorough job, pouring out information non-stop. The amount to absorb in a three-hour tour is quite bewildering. Details become confused. This chapter summarises much of the regular itinerary – apart from Kremlin and Red Square, described in the previous section. If you want to return to any specific site, the nearest Metro station is mentioned in the text.

The Central Squares

A semi-circular inner hub road encloses the Kremlin and Red Square. From the Kammenyi Bridge on the Moskva River, the boulevard sweeps round as Marx Prospekt, linking the principal central squares. Moscow's main radial highways spin off from Marx Prospekt, and many of the city's most important monuments are located along this extremely broad avenue.

Start from opposite the Kremlin's Borovitsky Gate. On the left – occupying the entire city block from Frunze Street to Kalinin Prospekt – are the buildings of the **Lenin Library**. With 22 reading rooms and an ever-increasing 37 million books, it's the world's third largest library after British Museum and Library of Congress. (Metro: Biblioteka Im. Lenina and Kalininskaya.)

50th Anniversary of October Square (formerly Manege Square)

Then comes a mustard-coloured classical building, which is the **Central Exhibition Hall**, formerly a military riding school called *Manege*. It was built in 1825 to celebrate the Russian defeat of Napoleon in 1812. Further along, on the left, is the original classical-style **Moscow University** – in enormous contrast to the modern skyscraper University out on Lenin Hills. All this huge square is packed on November 7 with troops and their hardware for the October Parade through Red Square. Across to the Kremlin walls is Alexander Gardens and the Tomb of the Unknown Soldier. Ahead is *Moskva Hotel*,

41

with Gorky Street to the left, and Red Square to the right. A pedestrian underpass is the only way to cross without policemen whistling at you.

Revolution Square

Moscow Hotel separates Karl Marx Prospekt from Revolution Square. Alongside the 11-storey **Gosplan Building**, headquarters of State Planning, is **Trade Union House** by the corner of Pushkin Street. The name sounds rather down-to-earth, but the building was originally an aristocratic club, allocated to the trade unions in 1919. Lenin made many speeches there. Today the main Hall of Columns is used for classical music concerts in a magnificent setting.

Over on Revolution Square is **Lenin Museum**. By the Metro station, Revolution Square merges with Sverdlov Square.

Sverdlov Square

Pre-1917, this was **Theatre Square**. The pink and white building is the **Bolshoi Theatre**, home of the world-famed opera and ballet company. Built in 19th-century neo-classical style, the eight-columned portico is surmounted by a replica of the quadriga like in St Mark's Square, Venice – four horses pulling a chariot of Apollo. Look towards the Bolshoi: left-hand corner of the Square is the charming yellow and white **Children's Theatre**; centre is a statue of Karl Marx; right is the **Maly Theatre** (meaning 'small', in contrast to Bolshoi which is 'big').

Dzerzhinsky Square

Next along Karl Marx Prospekt is Dzerzhinsky Square, named after the security chief – statue in the centre – who founded the Cheka, now better known as the KGB. The building to the left with arched windows is **Detskiy Mir** – Children's World – the department store for children. Opposite is the **Lubyanka**, a former insurance company office block which is **KGB headquarters**. (Metro: Ploshchad Dzerzhinsky.)

Novaya Square and Staraya Square

Changing direction, rightwards, the highway turns into New (Novaya) and Old (Staraya) Squares which are really more like streets. Left is the **Polytechnic Museum**; right is **Museum of the History and Reconstruction of Moscow**. Both are worth visiting, if you have time.

Along Staraya Square, watch for the green and yellow building on the right. That's where Mikhail Gorbachev works, as secretary to the **Central Committee of the Communist Party**.

Across the River Moskva is a waterfront district of former merchant houses, where their owners stored goods on the ground floors, and lived above. Several churches are active in this area. Along Maurice Thorez Embankment is the **British Embassy**, a beautiful building with a superb view of the Kremlin.

Kalinin Prospekt

Kalinin Avenue is a showpiece of Moscow's postwar reconstruction. Thirty years ago, the area was a forest of cranes, as old buildings were demolished to make room for this prestigious highway. It's the grand entry into central Moscow from Western Europe and Poland, along the M1 motorway. Altogether 26 government ministries are spread along the avenue, with cafés, restaurants and shops at street level.

Starting from the Lenin Library at the Kremlin end of Kalinin Prospekt, no. 14 is the **House of Friendship** (Dom Druzhby) where meetings can be arranged with Soviet people. At Arbatskaya Square (with a Metro) is the beginning of **Arbat Street**, now a pedestrian precinct. Some of old-time Moscow is preserved in the side-alleys.

Kalinin Prospekt ends dramatically with one of Stalin's wedding-cake skyscrapers – the **Hotel Ukraine**, which has an entrance lobby like Grand Central Station. Altogether, Moscow has seven of these wedding-cakes: two hotels, two ministries, two apartment blocks, and Moscow University on Lenin Hills.

Lenin Hills and Luzhiniki Park

The most direct route from the Kremlin to the Lenin Hills runs south-west along Volkhonka Street past the **Pushkin Museum of Fine Art** on the right, and the open-air **Moscow Swimming Baths** on the left. Here's the beginning – right – of the **Boulevard Ring** which loops around the inner heart of Moscow. (Metro: Kropotkinskaya.) Several more museums are located in the area along Kropotkinskaya Street, including **Pushkin House** and **Tolstoy Museum**. The route crosses the principal inner ring road called the Gardens Ring.

At the beginning of a park is a fine monument to Tolstoy, looking very stern. He lived close by in a house preserved as another Tolstoy Museum. The area is thick with medical institutions. Ahead is **Novodevichy Convent** (see section 2.7).

Rearing high above the river is Moscow's tallest building – the **University** on Lenin Hills, built 1953 in Stalin's favourite style of wedding-cake. Towers are silhouetted against the clouds. Thirty-two storeys high, this enormous building accommodates around 30,000 students in the University's 16 departments. The campus is spread over 750 acres. (Metro: Universitet.)

Close by is an observation platform which offers a splendid panorama of Moscow. Intourist sightseeing coaches normally stop at the viewpoint by **Luzhnikovski Bridge**, close to the charming 18th-century **Holy Trinity Church**. This is a functioning church with weekday services at 8 and 17 hrs; and on Sundays and festival days at 7, 10 and 17 hrs.

Inside the curve of Moskva River is the 100,000-capacity Central Lenin Stadium which is part of the **Luzhiniki Sports Complex**, where the 1980 Olympics were held. Luzhiniki Park includes tennis courts, the Swimming Stadium and numerous other sport facilities to make up the largest athletics ensemble in Europe. On the Lenin Hills' side of the river is a ski-jump with artificial coating so that wintersport fanatics can train even in summer. (Metro: Leninskiye Gory.)

Moscow Film Studios are located south of the river. For film buffs, this is where the famous Eisenstein films – like *Battleship Potemkin* – were made.

2.6 A Stroll Down Gorky Street

On a brief visit to Moscow, most of your time will be filled with city tours and excursions. But Moscow is also full of rewarding impressions for those who go wandering by themselves on foot. There are dozens of possibilities for strolling around, looking more closely at anything that catches your eye. For a sample, take a stroll down Gorky Street for a combination of shop-gazing with light sightseeing. This main avenue was renamed in 1917 after the renowned writer, Maxim Gorky.

Start from **Pushkin Square** (Metro: Pushkinskaya), and it's downhill all the way. For the big parades of May 1 and November 7, this is the line of march towards Red Square and the Kremlin at the bottom. Notice the enormous width of the road. The widening scheme was among Moscow's major reconstruction projects of the 1930's. Buildings worth preserving were simply moved as much as 50 yards back from their original position.

Pushkin Square is a pleasant little park, with benches beneath the trees, and pigeons to feed. It forms part of the **Boulevard Ring** which makes a five-mile circle of greenery around the centre of town. The **Pushkin Statue** in tribute to Russia's favourite national poet was erected in 1880. It's a popular meeting-place, particularly for dissidents who wish to protest about something. Around this square is the Fleet Street of Moscow, with editorial offices of the Novosti Press Agency, Tass News Agency, Izvestiya (with architecture in the 'Constructivist' style), Moscow News and other newspapers.

Steps lead to a very large 3,000-seat capacity cinema called Rossiya, vintage 1961. When they were showing *King Kong*, it was billed as a 'fantastic film'.

Just down Gorky Street, at number 14 on the left-hand side, is **Gastronom No. 1** – Moscow's most famous food store – a bizarre survival from pre-Revolutionary days. Muscovites queue at sausage and canned meat counters, beneath enormous chandeliers. Walls and ceilings are decorated with arabesques, pillars and gilded stucco-work. The aroma of grinding coffee beans mingles with that of smoked fish. Don't miss it! Like most food shops, Gastronom No. 1 is open from 8 to 20 hrs every day including Sundays.

A little further down Gorky Street is a window display that is just lace curtains, and the Russian word **Perfumery**. Plainly the art of window-dressing has not yet even reached infancy. But then you come to a national costume shop, and a store that specialises in crystal glass and paste jewellery – and both have reasonably attractive displays.

Drop in to the bread shop. See how Russians test each loaf before buying, using a kind of spoon to check the crust for firmness. Consider the oddity of having a baker's shop on the city's most prestigious street, like Fifth Avenue. But this simple bread-shop is wood-panelled, with chandeliers and a fancy stucco ceiling. It also doubles as a cafeteria – glass of tea 3 kopeks, coffee 23 kopeks. Alongside the automated cash register is an abacus in case of electronic failure.

Then, on both sides of the road, two very large bookstores occupy considerable prime frontage. Moskva Knigi – **Moscow Books** – extends for a city block. In the English-language section are books with snappy titles like 'The Undying Tradition of Folk Handicrafts in the Mid-Volga Region'.

Opposite is Druzhba – Friendship – which specialises in books from Communist-bloc countries. Art books are extremely good value. If you want to check out both sides of the street, use the pedestrian underpass. Traffic moves extremely fast. The official speed limit is 37 mph, but most drivers go faster.

Just past the Moskva Knigi bookshop is the **Square of the Soviets**, dominated by a statue of Yuri Dolgoruky, nicknamed Yuri the Long-Arm, who founded Moscow eight centuries ago. Seated on a horse, he stretches out his arm as though waiting for a tailor to come and measure it for length.

Facing him is the purple-red **City Hall** – Mossoviet, the meeting place of the Moscow Soviet. Dating from 1782, it was originally the palace of Moscow's Governor-General. After 1917, Lenin often spoke from the balcony above the front door. To the right, a metal plaque shows Lenin in oratorical mode. This building was lifted back 45 feet during the 1930's road-widening.

If you photograph Yuri the Long-Arm from behind, so that his arm is silhouetted against the sky, facing and pointing down towards Lenin's plaque on the City Hall building, then you'll never forget these little snippets of history.

Go to the end of the little park, and you'll find another statue of Lenin, in characteristic Thinker pose. That is highly apropriate, as he is seated in front of the **Lenin Institute** – the Soviet Union's main centre for Leninist and Marxist studies.

Back to Gorky Street: next, on your right, are two VIP apartment buildings. The massive granite blocks at street level were originally quarried on Hitler's orders, to build a Victory Monument to celebrate the downfall of Moscow. The ready-hewn stone came useful in postwar reconstruction.

Go through the archway, down Nezhdanovoy Street where several of the blocks of flats were built in 1920's for theatrical folk. If it's near to religious service time, you could visit golden-domed 17th-century **St Nicholas**, which is a functioning church.

Turn back to Gorky Street. Immediately opposite is a large Gastronom self-service store. It's worth looking around, if only to marvel at the lack of choice. Away on the next corner, right, is the **Central Telegraph Office**, with the time in lights. Gorky Street ends with Intourist Hotel rising skywards, with Prospekt Marksa Metro station below. To reach Red Square, take the pedestrian underpass.

2.7   Take A Trip

So many interesting places to visit! Which to choose? Here are some of the possibilities.

In Moscow

River Trip and Gorky Park

An ideal combination: a trip on the Moskva River, and a visit to Gorky Park.

If you're starting from the jetty near Kievsky Station, you have a view along to Moscow University with Novodevichy Convent to the left. Occasionally a hydrofoil comes rocketing along. There's a surprising amount of greenery in this area, with Luzhniki Park sports complex on one side, and woodlands rising opposite on the Lenin Hills.

Gorky Park is officially called the Central Park of Culture and Leisure. It's a lively 680-acre amusement park with fountains, Ferris wheel, boating lakes, children's funfair, open-air theatre, dancing and chess. It's worth a visit, to see another side of how Muscovites enjoy themselves. (Metro: Park Kultury and walk across Krymsky Bridge; or Oktabrskaya.)

Novodevichy Convent

This convent from the 16th century was built like a fortress, to protect the approaches to Moscow. Outside walls vary from 16 to 40 feet high, and are up to 20 feet thick. The building survived two invasions by the Crimean Tatars. Napoleon gave orders for the Convent to be blown up, but some remaining nuns persuaded the French troops to refrain.

The institution was always closely connected with the Tsar's court and with noble families. As portrayed in Mussorgsky's opera, in 1598 Boris Godunov was here invited by the Muscovites to be Tsar. Within the walls is Smolensky Cathedral, built 1524. The entire group of buildings is an architectural gem. In the cemetery are buried some of the greatest Russian personalities: leading writers, musicians, painters and statesmen.

On Intourist circuits, a shopping stop is usually made at the neighbouring Beriozka store.

Metro Tour

Understandably, Muscovites take pride in their Metro – not just for its efficiency, but also for the architectural design and decoration of each station. You can hop in and out of trains by yourself, to admire the art-work. But Intourist offer a more organised approach, taking groups on a sightseeing tour of the principal stations.

Each one is something different. Ploshchad Sverdlova, for instance, is decorated like a theatre, to reflect its proximity to the Bolshoi.

Mayakovskaya, dedicated to a Soviet poet, shimmers with stainless steel. In 1941 a major Party meeting was held in this deep-underground station and addressed by Stalin, while Nazi troops were shelling the city. Significantly, work continued on the Metro even throughout the war.

Belorusskaya Station features white marble from the Urals. There's a dramatic sculpture in socialist realism style – a monument to the Partisans of Belorussia. Ceilings are decorated with Belorussian mosaics.

Komsomol'skaya is dedicated to the young people who helped build the Metro. It looks more like a ballroom than a subway station. Mosaics illustrate events from the history of the Soviet Union.

The tour also serves as an introductory course on using the Metro by yourself.

Outside Moscow

Travel outside Moscow should be done in conjunction with Intourist, owing to visa restrictions.

Kolomenskoye

Overlooking the Moskva River south of Moscow, this estate was formerly a summer residence of the Czars. As well as an exhibition of Russian applied art, there is an interesting collection of Russian architecture, including an old Russian 'tent' style church built in 1532, and the log cabin in which Peter I was born. The estate is also famed for its grove of ancient oaks, with trees that are 600-800 years old.

Zagorsk

This is a full-day excursion to an old Russian town 45 miles northeast of Moscow. Here you will find a priceless collection of treasures from the 15th to 17th centuries. The famous Trinity Monastery of St Sergius, built in 1340, was the core of this fortress city. First it resisted Tatar invasions, and then a 16-month seige by Poles and Lithuanians.

Zagorsk was a major centre of learning and culture – second only to Kiev – and today remains the centre of Russian orthodoxy. The journey passes many collective farms and workers' villages, which form a striking contrast to the busy, built-up capital.

2.8 *Selection of Museums and Galleries*

The following is a small selection of Moscow's Museums, Exhibitions and Galleries which have a specialized appeal. Please ask your representative if you require any further details. Check on opening times, which may change – especially for the smaller collections. Many museums close for a day, towards the end of each month.

USSR Exhibition of Economic Achievements (VDNKh for short)

Location: In northern Moscow, up Mira Prospekt (motorway M2), opposite Cosmos Hotel
Nearest Metro: VDNKh (pronounced vay-day-en-kha)
Open: Grounds open daily 9.45 until 22 hrs, or until 23 hrs on Saturday and Sunday; Pavilions close at 19 hrs. Entrance 30 kopeks. Easily visited on an Intourist excursion.

A 750-acre park with some 100,000 exhibits on show, in over 80 large pavilions. Every aspect of the Soviet economy is displayed, from industry and agriculture to atomic energy and astronautics. An obelisk, shaped like an arrow, soars 315 feet into the sky to commemorate Soviet achievements in space.

For 10 kopeks you can take an overall ride around the

grounds on a 40-seater open trolley, bus-stopping at varied locations. Many visitors disembark at Kosmos, devoted to space exploration – easily recognised by a spacecraft in the middle of Industry Square, ringed by technology pavilions.

You can inspect a complete range of satellites, with their solar panels stretched out like wings. From there, you can gradually work back to the entrance, dropping in to any pavilions that catch your eye.

On a less technical basis, a visit to VDNKh is like a mini-tour of the Soviet Union, complete with ethnic restaurants, statues and fountains. You can survey the agricultural scene in all its continent-wide diversity, look at developments in Siberia or consider the very modest progress in desk-top computers. Russian tourists and Muscovite families find it just as fascinating for a day out. If you're pressed for time, at least give it a few hours.

Arts and Cultural Museums

Pushkin Museum of Fine Art

Location: 12 Ulitsa Volkhonka – a few blocks west of the southwest corner of the Kremlin, on Volkhonka Street across from Moscow Open-Air Swimming Pool.
Nearest Metro: Kropotkinskaya
Open: Daily except Tuesday, 10-20 hrs.

After the Hermitage in Leningrad, the Pushkin Museum has the richest collection of foreign art in the Soviet Union, covering ancient times to the 20th century. It includes antiquities from Egypt, Assyria, Babylon and Rome and works by west-European painters. All the Italian, Flemish, Dutch and Spanish schools are well represented.

But the Pushkin Museum's international renown comes particularly from its great collection of French Impressionists and Post-Impressionists – Cézanne, Monet, Manet, Gauguin, Matisse and early Picasso. If time is short, head straight for Rooms 17 to 23 on the first floor.

Alexander Pushkin Museum

Location 12/2 Kropotkin Street
Nearest Metro: Kropotkinskaya
Open: Daily except Monday

Don't confuse this literary museum with the Pushkin Museum of Fine Art, though the two are only a few blocks apart. It's a timber house of 1814 vintage, devoted to the life and works of Russia's national poet.

Museum of Oriental Art

Location: 12a Suvorovsky Boulevard
Nearest Metro: Arbatskaya
Open: Daily except Monday, 11-19 hrs.

Folk arts and crafts of many Eastern countries – particularly China, Japan, India and including the Asian republics of the Soviet Union.

Ostankino Palace – Museum of Serf Art

Location: 5 Pervaya Ostankinskaya Ulitsa – northern Moscow, in the grounds of Dzerzhinsky Park, west of the Exhibition of Economic Achievements of the USSR (VDNKh). It faces the 1650-ft TV mast called Ostankino Tower, which you can hardly miss!
Nearest Metro: VDNKh

This attractive timber palace was entirely designed and built by serf labour in 1792-98, and now houses a rich collection of serf art including wood carvings and parquetry. The owner of the palace was a connoisseur of music and theatre. From his thousands of serfs he picked a talented company of 200 actors, actresses, dancers and musicians who gave lavish performances in the purpose-built theatre.

In the park grounds are the Botanic Gardens of the Academy of Sciences.

Museum of Folk Art

Location: 7 Ulitsa Stanislaskogo (a turning off Gorky Street, further up from the City Soviet building)
Nearest Metro: Pushkinskaya or Marx Prospekt
Open: Daily except Monday
Folk art from 17th century onwards.

Bakhrushin Central Theatre Museum

Location: 31/12 Ulitsa Bakhrushina (south of Moskva River, near Paveletskiy Station)
Nearest Metro: Paveletskaya
Open: Daily except Tuesday

For theatre buffs: everything about the Russian stage – drama, opera, ballet – from 18th century till modern times. Costumes, programmes, posters, famous actors, and over 200,000 photos.

Glinka Museum of Musical Culture

Location: 4 Ulitsa Fadeyeva
Nearest Metro: Nayakovskaya or Novoslobodskaya

A remarkable collection of musical instruments; and musical scores and letters of the great composers of 19th and 20th centuries, Russian and west European.

Tolstoy House-Museum in Khamovniki

Location: 21 Ulitsa Lva Tolstogo (Leo Tolstoy Street)
Nearest Metro: Park Kultury
Open: Daily except Monday, 10-16 hrs.

Tolstoy's town house and grounds, where he spent his

winters from 1882 till 1901. His simple study is preserved, where he wrote *Resurrection*, *The Death of Ivan Ilyich* and other major works.

Mayakovsky Museum

Location: 3/6 Proyezd Serova (Serov Passage). On the corner of Dzerzhinsky Square and Kirov Street
Nearest Metro: Dzerzhinskaya
Open: Monday and Thursday 12-20 hrs; Tuesday and Friday-Sunday 10-18 hrs; closed Wednesday.

In this apartment worked Mayakovsky – 'the poet of the Revolution' – from 1919 until he mysteriously shot himself in 1930, aged 37. (Another Mayakovsky House-Museum is located at 26 Krasnaya Presnaya Ulitsa – Metro: Krasnopresnenkaya.)

Chekhov House Museum

Location: 6 Sadovaya-Kudrinskaya Ulitsa (on the Garden Ring Road)
Nearest Metro: Barrikadnaya
Open: Tuesday, Thursday, Saturday and Sunday 11-18 hrs; Wednesday and Friday 14-21 hrs.

The house of Anton Chekhov, who started writing while a medical student at Moscow University. The museum is furnished in style appropriate to the period 1886–1890, when Chekhov lived here.

Maxim Gorky Museum

Location: 25a Ulitsa Vorovskogo (near Kalinin Prospekt)
Nearest Metro: Arbatskaya
Open: Daily except Monday

A detailed literary museum covering the work of Maxim Gorky (1868–1936).

History Museums

Soviet Armed Forces Museum

Location: 2 Ulitsa Sovetskoi Armii (behind the Soviet Army Theatre at Kommuny Ploshchad, and close to Soviet Army HQ)
Nearest Metro: Mira Prospekt
Open: Tuesday and Friday-Sunday 10-17 hrs; Wednesday and Thursday 13-20 hrs. Closed Monday.

Covers history and development of Soviet armed forces since 1917, with considerable coverage of World War II battles. Also displayed are exhibits from the American U-2 reconnaissance plane flown by Francis Gary Powers and brought down over Siberia in 1960.

Battle of Borodino Panorama-Museum

Location: 38 Kutuzovsky Prospekt (a circular blue building)

Nearest Metro: Kutuzovskaya
Open: Daily except Friday 9.30-20 hrs in summer; 10.30-19 hrs in winter.

Ringside view of the inconclusive battle of Borodino, fought 70 miles west of Moscow in August 1812 between Napoleon's army and the Russian forces commanded by General Kutuzov. (Read all about it, in Tolstoy's *War and Peace*.) The circular painting is almost 400 feet long, 50 feet high.

Central Lenin Museum

Location: 2 Ploshchad Revolyutsii (opposite Moscow Hotel, on Revolution Square)
Nearest Metro: Prospekt Marksa or Ploshchad Revolyutsii
Open: Daily except Monday 10-19 hrs.

Devoted to the life and work of Lenin – revolutionary thinker and founder of the Soviet State. A half-hour Russian-language film includes historic footage. Thirty four rooms are packed with exhibits that give complete coverage of Lenin's action-packed career. There's a replica of Lenin's study in the Kremlin. Russian visitors particularly admire his 1919 Rolls-Royce Silver Ghost.

Karl Marx and Friedrich Engels Museum

Location: 5 Ulitsa Marksai Engelsa (Marx-Engels Street, behind the Pushkin Fine Arts Museum)
Nearest Metro: Kropotkinskaya
Open: Tuesday, Wednesday and Friday 12-19 hrs; Thursday, Saturday and Sunday 11-18 hrs.

Exhibits relating to the life and work of Karl Marx and Friedrich Engels, the pioneers of Communist theory.

Red Presnya (Krasnaya Presnya) Museum

Location: 4 Ulitsa Bolshevistkaya (Bolshevik Street)
Nearest Metro: Krasnopresnenkaya

A wooden building which was a Bolshevik headquarters in 1917, now devoted to the first Russian revolution of 1905–1907.

Central Museum of the Revolution

Location: 21 Gorky Street (near Mayakovsky Square)
Nearest Metro: Mayakovskaya
Open: Tuesday and Wednesday 12-20 hrs; Thursday and Sunday 10-18 hrs; Friday 11-19 hrs.

Formerly the English Club with gateway guarded by stone lions, this museum displays relics, photographs and documents of the 1905 Revolution, the February revolt of 1917, and the October Revolution that followed it.

2.9 Shopping

Most visitors to Moscow make the bulk of their purchases in the Beriozka hard-currency stores. However, for a few items – such as books, sheet music, posters and gramophone records – choice may be wider in specialized shops. Otherwise, shop-gazing is merely to satisfy curiosity, not with any serious expectation of finding anything worth buying.

Beriozka Stores

The best Beriozka is at Hotel Rossiya. Another very good one is opposite the Novodevichy Convent (shopping time is often included on tours to the Convent). Smaller Beriozkas are located in the Hotel National (just around the corner from Intourist Hotel), and in Hotel Cosmos.

GUM

An average quarter-million customers elbow through the doors of GUM every weekday, storming the hundreds of sales counters. Bemused tourists wander in from Red Square, finding the whole thing fascinating.

There are three shopping streets, with individual shops each side, on two levels. Little bridges connect the upper levels. Most of the shops are in clothing business. Just walk in and look around. Nobody will pressure you into buying. Each store is quite separate from its neighbour. The central aisle has a fountain where lost souls are re-united with their loved ones, eating ice cream while they wait.

Most interesting is to stroll through the Gastronom food department on the ground floor – nearest to Red Square side. They sell tinned fish and other goodies amid a remarkable setting of chandeliers, ornamentation and ceiling mirrors.

Try going latish in the evening, perhaps after dinner, when the crowds are thinning. GUM closes at 21 hrs. The final hour would give enough time to explore without being trampled underfoot.

Other Stores to Visit

Detskiy Mir (Children's World) – 2 Marx Prospekt. A children's department store, with toys of every description.

Dom Knigi (The House of Books) – 26 Kalinin Prospekt. Is particularly good for books on art and architecture, some translations of Russian classics, and eye-catching posters.

Melodiya – 40 Kalinin Prospekt – just along the road from Dom Knigi. If you're interested in recorded music, here's a bargain spot – not just for Soviet recordings, but also those from other east-European nations.

2.10 Eating Out in Moscow

Restaurant Guide

Considering that Moscow is a major world capital, characteristic restaurants are in very short supply. Here's a recommended list, for which reservations can be made through Intourist. Ask your tour-operator representative for any further details.

Aragvi

16 Gorky Street
Offering 30 of the best known Georgian dishes: sulguni cheese, shashlik, chicken zatsivi smothered in walnut sauce, boiled sturgeon, chicken tabako.
  Georgian wines: Tsinandali, Mukuzani, Kakhetia.

Uzbekistan

29 Neglinnaya Street
Tkhum-dulma (boiled egg within fried meat patty), mustava (rice soup with meat), maniar (broth with minced meat and egg), Uzbek shashlik – diced meat, cooked over charcoal.
  Wines: Aleatiko and Uzbekistan.

Baku

24 Gorky Street
Azerbaijan dishes – specialising in up to 20 different kinds of Pilav. Nut soup with chicken, shashlik, basturma, golubtsky (minced meat and rice cooked in vine leaves), nakurma (roast lamb with pomegranates).
  Wines: Matrassa and Shamkhor; Akstafa (dessert wine).

Ararat

4 Neglinnaya Street
Armenian dishes: Solyanka Armenian style, Yerevan bozbash, trout, shashlik and Chebureks (deep fried meat pies).
  Beverages include pungent Armenian brandies, muscats and sherry.

Slaviansky Bazaar

17, 25th October Street
Russian style cuisine accompanied by an orchestra and cabaret. Genuine Russian atmosphere.

Arbat

29 Kalinin Prospekt
Russian style cuisine. It has an orchestra, and there is a large dance area. A good atmosphere of 'Russians at Play'.

54

Cooperatives Restaurants

There are many good restaurants which offer excellent food and service. They are sometimes slightly more expensive, but it's worth paying the extra for the difference in quality.

2.11 Moscow by Night

For all kinds of classical music, Moscow is a year-round destination. But the music-lover should particularly note two major annual arts festivals: 'Russian Winter' from 25 December to 5 January; and 'Moscow Stars' from 5 to 13 May.

Opera and Ballet

Every visitor to Moscow should see a performance of opera or ballet. Theatres are always packed. If the Bolshoi companies are away on world tours, groups from other Soviet cities can be of almost equal calibre. Make your reservations at the first opportunity. Performances are given either at the historic Bolshoi Theatre, or at the 6,000-seat Palace of Congresses in the Kremlin.

Other theatres to visit are the Stanislavsky and Nemirovich-Danchenko Musical Theatre which stages ballet and opera; and the Moscow Operetta Theatre for light opera and musical comedy.

Circus

Another 'must' is the Moscow State Circus – excellent entertainment of the highest standard with the cream of Soviet performers. If the State Circus is on tour, a more modest but traditional alternative is available in the tented circus in Gorky Park. Or you could save a circus visit till Leningrad, which also offers a high calibre show.

Concerts and Folklore Shows

Moscow rates very high among world capitals of music. Standards are superb. Every week there's wide choice of classical concerts given by various national and city ensembles. In addition, there are always major folk-music companies in town, such as the Pyatnitsky Choir or the brilliant Don Cossack group.

Concerts are held in the famous Tchaikovsky Conservatoire, where so many of the greatest Russian artistes have performed; in Tchaikovsky Concert Hall; and in the Hall of Columns, which is a glittering survival from the vanished era of aristocracy.

Straight Theatre

If you understand Russian, and would like to see a

production in Russian, your hotel will have a list of plays that are currently being presented. The Moscow Arts Theatre is the shrine of Stanislavsky, specializing in the great classics – particularly Chekhov.

Out of the 30 theatres in Moscow, five are for children. The Puppet Theatre on Spartakovskaya Street can give pleasure to adults.

Evening on Arbat Street

Here's a fascinating development since 1986: almost a mile of street entertainment along Arbat Street (from Arbatskaya Square to Smolenskaya Square, with a Metro station at each end).

It's a pedestrian precinct with street performers along the entire distance, mainly from about 7 p.m. until lights-out at 11. The closest parallel is to London's Covent Garden.

At the Kalinin Street end, by Arbatskaya Square, scores of instant-portrait artists of varying styles and skill are surrounded by attentive onlookers. Other artists prefer the underpass beneath Kalinin Street. A typical black-and-white portrait is offered at five roubles, done in 15 to 20 minutes. Painters display finished canvases.

Close by, poets recite their verses to an appreciative audience. Others more shyly hang poems on a wall, individually typed out, dated and signed. A neat idea to get your works read and circulated, if not published!

Further along, and it's musicians all the way: individual ballad-singers, small groups, traditional and folklore, right through to Heavy Metal. Musicians come here from all parts of the Soviet Union. Some musicians offer songs with a satirical bite. Listeners concentrate on the words, and occasionally burst into laughter or applause. Other groups are into folk music, with a lively audience that breaks into song and dance.

Altogether, it's a fun place for seeing mostly younger Russians enjoying an evening out, at minimal cost – just coins in the hat to show appreciation. It's delightful for an after-dinner stroll.

The Arbat development has proved so popular that another street has recently been pedestrianized, with the same idea of providing an informal venue for street entertainment – Sretenka Ulice (at bottom end of Mira Prospekt, by Kolchoznaya Metro station). Ask first, whether it can rival Arbat Street.

Chapter Three

3.1 Leningrad – Window on the West

First impressions are always the most memorable. Wintertime, as you travel from Leningrad airport into a snow-covered city, you possibly expect something drab and grey. Instead, the first delighted impression is of *colour*.

Floodlit public buildings are brightly painted in birthday-cake style: blue and white, yellow, green and red. The golden domes and spires of cathedrals and churches dominate the skyline. In central Leningrad, there's hardly a single building in the 20th-century international idiom of steel, glass and concrete.

Leningrad – a capital city founded by Peter the Great in the early 18th century to give Russia a 'window on the west' – has preserved its original layout and architectural style. Leningrad is built astride several branches of the River Neva, with a hundred islands, canals and something like 400 ornamental wrought-iron bridges. From its foundation, St Petersburg was laid out spaciously with broad squares, wide boulevards and dozens of little parks. In the centre, no building was permitted above three storeys high, to avoid overtopping the Winter Palace.

To beautify the capital, the Tsars imported foreign advisers. Italian architects brought the gaiety of Mediterranean colours to the sun-starved city. Palaces, churches and mansions were built in light-hearted baroque, especially by Rastrelli and his pupils.

Soviet policy is to conserve this appearance. In truth, older town houses are inconvenient by 20th-century standards. There has been debate on whether to tear the whole lot down, and build anew with more lasting materials. That has been the policy in Moscow, where some 90 per cent of buildings date from post-1918. But the consensus in Leningrad is to preserve the city's original appearance, even if that is uneconomic. Stately 19th-century merchant houses have been converted to flats, with interiors gutted and re-fitted to suit modern life-styles.

But constant renovation is still needed to preserve these traditional Leningrad buildings. The climate is unhelpful. The freezing winter flakes away the surfaces of colour-

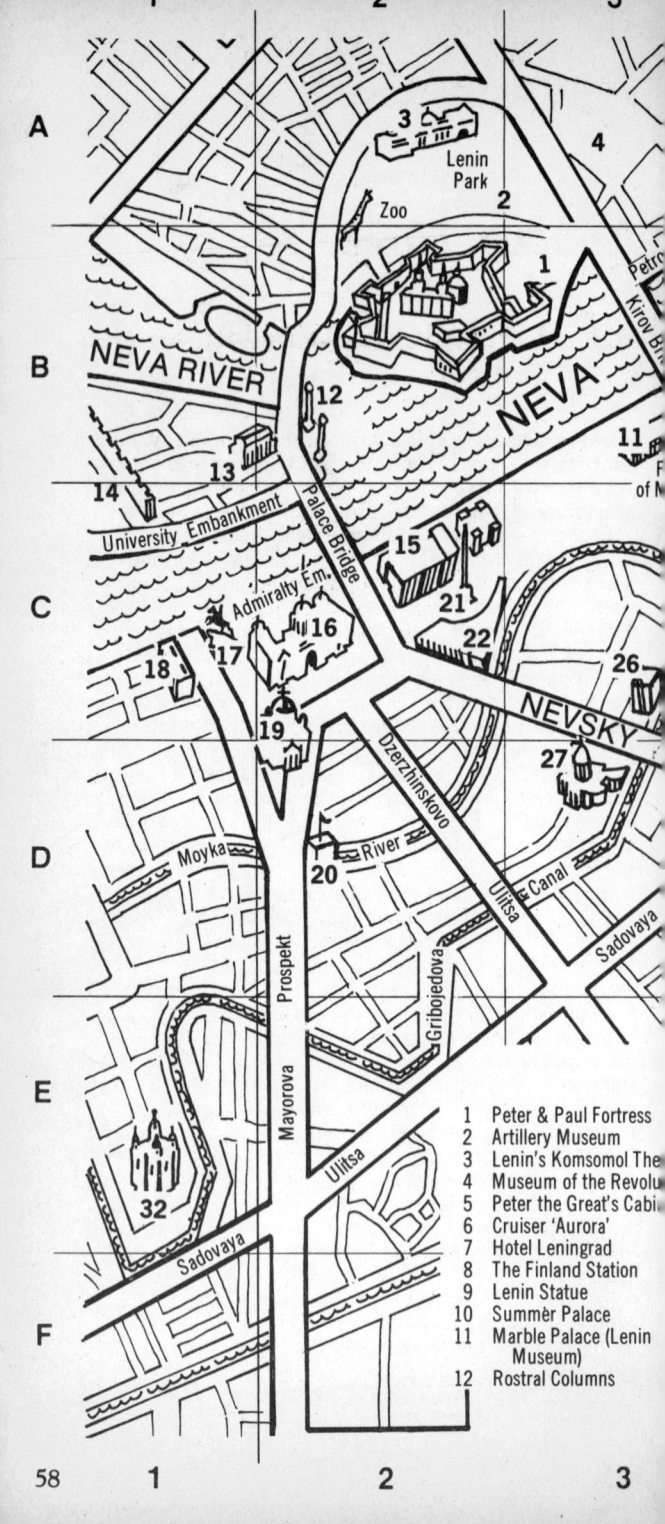

1 Peter & Paul Fortress
2 Artillery Museum
3 Lenin's Komsomol The
4 Museum of the Revolu
5 Peter the Great's Cabi
6 Cruiser 'Aurora'
7 Hotel Leningrad
8 The Finland Station
9 Lenin Statue
10 Summer Palace
11 Marble Palace (Lenin
   Museum)
12 Rostral Columns

3	Naval Museum	23	Church of the Resurrection
4	Mendeleyev Line	24	Russian Museum
5	Winter Palace – The Hermitage	25	Engineer's Castle
6	Admiralty	26	St Catherine's Church
7	Bronze Horseman & Decembrists' Square	27	Kazan Cathedral
8	Senate House & Synod	28	Gostiny Dvor Department Store
9	St Isaac's Cathedral	29	Pushkin Theatre & Ostrovsky Square
0	Town Hall	30	Anichkov Bridge Sculptures
1	Palace Square & Triumphal Column	31	Moscow Station
2	General Staff HQ	32	St Nicholas Cathedral

washed facades, and the plaster needs regular attention. Public buildings must be repainted every two years.

As Russia's capital for 200 years, St Petersburg attracted all the best of cultural and intellectual life, and was the gateway for an interchange of ideas and fashions with western Europe. This was the home of the Academy of Sciences, Pushkin and Tchaikovsky – and also the centre of the political ferment that led to Revolution.

Many corners of present-day Leningrad can help you savour the atmosphere of that historical and cultural past. Any devotee of the 19th-century Russian writers – particularly Pushkin, Dostoevsky, Gogol and Turgenev, who all dwelt for some time in Leningrad – can relive much of the atmosphere they described. Amid that classical architecture, the pastel-coloured mansions and palaces, the little parks and canals, you can feel that the calendar has stopped for a hundred years.

Likewise, the music-lover can listen to Tchaikovsky, Glinka, Rimsky-Korsakov, Borodin and Mussorgsky, performed by artistes for whom the music is part of their blood-stream. Some of today's greatest ballet dancers are graduates of the Kirov. The Hermitage art collection in the former Winter Palace is among the world's greatest.

Leningrad's finest achievement has been the dedicated work of preserving the city's heritage. During the 900-day wartime siege, the city lost 650,000 population, while one third of the buildings were seriously damaged or destroyed. Today it's hard to believe that only a few houses escaped damage by bombing and shelling.

Most incredible has been the total rebuilding of the out-of-town summer palaces which were occupied and destroyed by Nazi troops. Inside those beautifully-restored palaces, the imagination can re-create all the aristocratic splendour of the former royal court. In contrast, across the river from the Winter Palace in central Leningrad stands the Peter and Paul Fortress, a Russian Bastille where political prisoners were kept, pending exile or execution.

To anyone tolerably familiar with the history of the Revolution, Leningrad offers extra fascination. You can stand in the Palace Square, scene of epoch-making events in 1905 and 1917; see the Smolny Institute, used as Lenin's Bolshevik HQ; go aboard the cruiser *Aurora*, which fired the shot to signal the storming of the Winter Palace. Visiting those locations first-hand, the drama all comes to life. For the politically-minded, Intourist arranges a Lenin Memorial Tour, which follows through Lenin's life and revolutionary activities in the months preceding the 1917 Revolution.

Today, Leningrad is the second largest city of the Soviet Union, with a population that has just reached 5 million. From 1712 till March 1918, it was the capital of Russia and still regards itself as being the cultural superior to

Moscow. Quite apart from thriving high-tech industry, Leningrad is a major centre of higher education. The intellectual atmosphere is invigorating, with a lively student population in a city which takes great pride in its universities.

3.2 Get Your Bearings in Leningrad

Start at the tip of Vasilyevsky Island, at the point called *The Strekla*. Here was the focal point of the original city planned by Peter the Great in 1703. To protect the site from the Swedes, the Peter and Paul Fortress was built – located ahead and to the left. The log cabin from which Peter directed operations was just past the present-day Kirov Bridge which lies straight ahead. On that same side of the river is anchored the cruiser *Aurora*, which fired the blank shot to inaugurate the 1917 October Revolution. Hotel Leningrad faces the *Aurora* across a side-stream of the River Neva. Ten minutes' walk from Hotel Leningrad is the Finland Station, where Lenin arrived from exile in 1917.

Just behind you, on the triangular tip of Vasilyevsky Island, Peter the Great laid out the central administration of his new city. Today the buildings are used as major museums, and for University and scientific institutions.

Now look right. The principal riverside building is the long blue and white facade of the Winter Palace, with statues of Roman gods and goddesses along the roof. That's the focal-point of tourist Leningrad: Palace Square and the Admiralty. Close by rises the golden dome of St. Isaac's Cathedral.

A majestic part of Peter's city planning was the layout of Nevsky Prospekt – a 3-mile avenue to link the Admiralty with the Alexander Nevsky Monastery, cutting across a U-bend of the River Neva. The area was marshy, needed draining. The water was channelled tidily into small rivers and canals, lined with granite.

Leningrad is sometimes described as 'the Venice of the North'. But perhaps a better comparison is Amsterdam (which Peter the Great knew from his travels) with its city-planned girdles of waterways. Moyka River is closest to the city-centre Admiralty and Winter Palace. Fontanka River, a five-mile semi-circle, formed the city boundary at the end of the 18th century. Many merchant houses and aristocratic mansions were built along these waterways, giving a unified character to the architecture.

Transport

Most city break visitors will want to make some use of public transport. From Hotel Leningrad the most convenient is tram no. 51 which terminates downtown near the Church of the Resurrection, within a few minutes' walk of Nevsky Prospekt. The Metro from Lenina Ploshchad (at the Finland Station) is only two stops to Vosstaniya Ploshchad (at Moscow Station), on Nevsky Prospekt. Number 2 yellow bus goes from the Finland Station to the Kazan Cathedral area. Five kopeks covers any single fare.

3.3   Basic Leningrad

Palace Square

The green and white Winter Palace dominates the city's architectural centre – Palace Square, the great focal-point of Russian history. For two centuries it saw all the pomp of the Court calendar, when the Romanovs ruled an expanding Empire. On this square, peaceful demonstrators were shot down in January 1905, when they came to petition the Tsar for better conditions. The 1905 Revolution was defeated. But October 1917 saw the start of the more permanent Bolshevik Revolution, when the Winter Palace was stormed.

The great semi-circular building opposite the Winter Palace was headquarters of the Tsarist General Staff. The yellow and white building is 650 yards long, with a triumphal arch crowned by a Victory Chariot, symbolizing Russia's triumph over Napoleon in 1812. The Alexander Column of polished red granite, in the centre of Palace Square, commemorates the same victory. On top is an angel, holding a cross and squashing a snake. Today, Palace Square is barred to traffic, leaving room for long queues that await admission to the Hermitage. As ever, Intourist groups are on the fast inside track.

The Hermitage

Open: daily except Mondays, 10.30-18.00 hrs (summer from 10.00 hrs).

Rated among the world's largest and richest art museums, the Hermitage collection is spread through 400 rooms of the Winter Palace and the adjoining Little Hermitage and Old Hermitage. Together, the buildings cover six acres. The main building dates principally from mid-18th century, when architect Rastrelli produced the fourth version of a Winter Palace, after the half-century's three previous attempts had failed to satisfy the reigning monarchs.

Many alterations were later made to the 1,000-room royal palace, especially after major fire damage in 1837. But the palace kept its Baroque style, with a majestic white marble staircase leading to the royal apartments. The rich decorations, sculptures, huge chandeliers and polished wooden floors have all been faithfully preserved by the Soviets, as part of the national heritage.

In 1767, the Little Hermitage was built, adjoining the Palace, to house the numerous art treasures which Empress Catherine the Great was rapidly adding to the basic nucleus formed by Peter the Great. His contribution was mainly of seascapes, and antique gold buckles from Siberia. Very soon the Old Hermitage was added, and extended further over the years. Each succeeding monarch made regular purchases to fill gaps. From 1917 many private galleries were nationalized, and the cream was added to the Hermitage museum – or shared with the Pushkin Gallery in Moscow.

A guided tour, lasting about 2½ hours, gives a general idea of what's on show, and where to find it. The sheer volume of exhibits is overwhelming. The Hermitage has 12 miles of galleries, and 3 million items – paintings, sculptures, furniture, gold and silverware, coins, porcelain and tapestries. If you studied each item for ten seconds, a complete tour would take 2½ years. Some 125 rooms and halls are devoted to West European art alone. Entire galleries are lined with Rembrandt, Raphael, Rubens, Van Dyke – every school of Western art, through to the Impressionists and Post-Impressionists. Among the riches is Europe's largest collection of Picasso's cubist period, and two superb rooms of Matisse and Gauguin.

The introductory guided tour can help you decide which areas interest you most, so you can return another day (or another year).

The Admiralty

Adjoining Palace Square is another integral part of the city's architectural centre: the Admiralty. It dates from the early days of St Petersburg, when Peter the Great was aiming to establish a Russian Navy. The site was originally a fortified shipyard. The present Admiralty building dates from early 19th century. The slender golden spire topped by a weathervane in full sail is the symbol of Leningrad, a popular subject for souvenirs.

Decembrists' Square

Next along the Admiralty Embankment is Decembrists' Square – so named in memory of the young officers of the Imperial Guard (all noblemen) who revolted against tsarist autocracy on 14 December 1825. Five ringleaders were hanged, and others exiled to Siberia.

Centre of the Square is the dramatic **Bronze Horseman** statue, rearing from a huge granite monolith. The horseman is Peter the Great, who makes a favourite photo subject for poetic-minded Russians with memories of *The Bronze Horseman* poem by Pushkin. The handsome 19th-century **Senate House** and the adjoining **Synod** fills the western side of the Square. The premises now house the **Central Historical Archive**.

At the riverside, admire the panoramic view across the Neva to the splendid line of Dutch-style buildings on the University Embankment of Vasilyevsky Island. From the right, there's the Zoological Museum, Anthropological Museum, Academy of Sciences, University buildings and Academy of Arts. Finally, just by the bridge, is the house where Pavlov lived – the dog man whose work on conditioned reflexes earned him a Nobel Prize in 1904. His flat is preserved as a museum.

Turning back, you see the golden dome of St Isaac's Cathedral, beyond the park with its green lawns and massed flower displays.

St Isaac's Cathedral

Location: Isaakiyevskaya Ploshchad (Isaac's Square)
Open: Daily except Wednesday, 11-18 hrs. Tuesday 11-16 hrs.

Fourth highest Cathedral in the world, St Isaac's was built in the 19th century, and lavishly decorated on every available square inch with nearly 500 paintings, sculptures and mosaics by celebrated Russian artists. You can climb to the dome for a panoramic view of Leningrad, but photos are not allowed.

St Isaac's Square

Facing the main entrance of St Isaac's Cathedral is City Hall, headquarters of the Leningrad City Soviet, with red flag flying and decorated with five medals given by Lenin. Formerly this was **Mariinsky Palace**, built 1844 for Maria, daughter of Tsar Nicholas I, whose equestrian statue rears up in the centre of the square.

Away in the south-western corner, at no. 5, is the **Museum of Musical Instruments** – one of the world's finest collections. It includes pianos that belonged to Russia's greatest composers.

From St Isaac's entrance, walk clockwise around the building. Some of the Cathedral's outside columns still are pock-marked from war damage. Further round, a corner of the square is occupied by a long creamy-green building in Greek temple style with an eight-column frontage. This was the 19th-century mansion of Prince Lobanov-Rostovsky. The park is Decembrists' Square (see above).

Arts Square

Located just north of Nevsky Prospekt, a city block away from Gostiny Dvor (the Merchants' Hall department store), the Arts Square is a cultural focal-point. The gardens centre on a **Pushkin statue**, erected in 1957. Surrounding buildings date from the 1830's, based on a master plan by architect Rossi. Dominating the north side of the square is the **Russian Museum**, originally built as the Grand Duke Mikhail Palace. On the opposite side is the **Maly Theatre** for Opera and Ballet.

In Brodskovo Street, which leads from the Arts Square to Nevsky Prospekt, facing Hotel Europe is the **Leningrad Philharmonic** concert hall. It was designed as a Gentlemen's Club, and its Large Hall became the venue for many classical concerts organised from 1859 by the Russian Musical Society.

In another street running into Arts Square – Inzhernernaya Ulitsa – is the **Ethnographic Museum**. An ochre building with white columns, the Museum is devoted to the art and life of the nationalities of the Soviet Union. (Open daily except Monday, 11-19 hrs).

The Russian Museum

Location: on Arts Square
Open: Daily except Tuesday, 11-18 hrs (summer from 10 hrs)

The Museum gives a complete picture of Russian art history across a thousand years, from 10th century to modern times, and covering all important periods and trends in the development of Russian art. It is particularly rich in icon paintings from 10th to 17th centuries. Make this your number two museum choice, after the Hermitage.

Field of Mars

Location: a park, just north of Arts Square, and south of Kirov Bridge

The Field of Mars is Leningrad's largest square, which originally was used for military parades. It contains a statue of Russia's great 18th-century General Suvorov; and also a memorial to revolutionaries who died in October 1917 and in the 1918–22 Civil War. The square has been converted into pleasant park gardens. The prettiest month is May, when the lilac trees are in full blossom.

From the Field of Mars you can see the **Church of the Resurrection**, built 1883-1907 to resemble St Basil's Cathedral in Moscow. The mosaic facade is under restoration, scheduled for completion in 1990. The building will then re-open as a museum.

Adjoining the Field of Mars – across Sadovaya Street – is the 30-acre Summer Garden and two-storeyed **Summer Palace**, built 1711 in Dutch style for Peter the Great's occasional use. Terracotta decorations on the facade celebrate Russian naval victories. Fountains are fed by the Fontanka River.

Vasilyevsky Island

During city sightseeing, most tour coaches make a

prolonged stop at the tip of Vasilyevsky Island, called **The Strelka,** which means The Arrow. See section 3.2 to identify details of the panorama, which makes an excellent photo-stop.

Dominating this viewpoint are the two **Rostral Columns** on Pushkin Square. They were designed as oil-fired beacons for ships arriving from the Baltic into the Merchants' Harbour. Rostral means prow, and symbolizes the port. All the monumental buildings in this area were intended for 18th-century government and business use, but their functions changed during the 19th century. Today, it's a district of museums, University buildings and academic institutes.

The central white-columned building on Pushkin Square was originally the Stock Exchange, now used as the **Central Naval Museum**. It contains over a thousand model ships. (Open: daily except Tuesday, 10.30-17.45 hrs.)

Next door, a former warehouse with yellow facade is the **Zoological Museum** which includes a Siberian mammoth in its very comprehensive collection. (Open: daily except Monday, 11-18 hrs.) On the northern side of the Stock Exchange, a similar warehouse now operates as the **Museum of Soil Science**.

Further round, on the Malaya Neva Embankment, the old Customs House has become the Institute of Russian Literature – also known as **Pushkin House**. The **Literary Museum** forms part of the Institute, and displays exhibits relating to most of the world-famed Russian writers, including Maxim Gorky, Gogol, Tolstoy, Turgenev and Dostoyevsky. (Open: daily except Monday and Tuesday, 11-18 hrs.)

Along the south-facing University Embankment – looking across the Neva River to the Admiralty – is the green and white **Museum of Ethnography and Anthropology**. It was purpose-built in 1718–34 as Russia's first public museum, to house Peter the Great's collection of Rarities, Curiosities and Monsters. A section is devoted to the Russian scientist Mikhail Lomonosov, who worked here from 1741 to 1765. (Open: Sunday-Thursday, 11-17 hrs.)

Behind all these museums, and along University Embankment, are the main buildings of Leningrad University. Among the former students were the chemist Dmitri Mendeleev, who tabled the periodic law of elements; physiologist Ivan Pavlov who worked with dogs on his theories of conditioned reflex; and Lenin who took an external law degree.

Leningrad University currently has 20,000 students and post-graduates. Courses last five years for full-time students; or six years for part-timers and those studying by correspondence.

Peter and Paul Fortress

Location: On opposite river bank to the Winter Palace
Open: daily except Wednesday, 11-18 hrs; Tuesday 11-16 hrs.

The foundation of St Petersburg dates from 27 May 1703, the official date of the founding of the Peter and Paul Fortress: an outpost to protect the new city from the Swedes.

In fact, the Swedes gave no trouble, and soon the fortress was more often used as a prison. Peter the Great's son Alexei was beaten to death for plotting against his father. In 19th century the Trubetskoy Bastion became a gaol for several generations of political prisoners. Dostoevsky was kept in the dungeon while awaiting execution (commuted to Siberian exile). The experience gave him material for *Crime and Punishment*. Lenin's elder brother was executed here in 1887. Maxim Gorky and Leon Trotsky were imprisoned after the 1905 uprising.

Today the fortress is a museum which includes a branch of the **Museum of the History of Leningrad**; and also a **Museum of St Petersburg Architecture**.

Within the grounds is the early 18th-century **Peter and Paul Cathedral**, whose slender golden spire is a major landmark. Most of the Russian Emperors and Empresses are buried here.

A working **Mint** was established in the Fortress in 1802. It continues to produce Soviet coins and medals, and also made the pennant left on the moon by a Russian spacecraft.

North of the Fortress, across the moat, is the **Artillery Museum** (open Wednesday to Sunday, 11.30-17.30 hrs). The grounds are bounded by Lenin Park, and the Zoo.

The Cruiser Aurora

Location: permanently moored by the Neva, facing Hotel Leningrad

The cruiser *Aurora* is historically famed for firing the blank round which signalled the storming of the Winter Palace on 25 October 1917 (or November 7, new style). The public can freely go aboard the vessel, which has been refitted to exhibit the crew's living quarters. On lower decks, the cruiser's history is graphically displayed with documents and photos. The ship was severely damaged in the Tsu-Shima battle against the Japanese in 1905. Soviet families enjoy having their photographs taken alongside the 6-inch bow gun which inaugurated the Revolution.

The spick-and-span blue building by the pier is a naval officers' academy.

Peter the Great's Cabin

Location: 3 Petrovsky Embankment – a few minutes' walk

from the *Aurora*
Open: daily except Tuesday, 11-19 hrs.

In 1703, when Peter the Great decided to build a new city, he needed living quarters from which to direct operations. In three days his soldiers erected this two-roomed log cabin. Eighty years later, to preserve the historic hut, an outer structure was built around the cabin which today is the only wooden building in Leningrad. It gives a close-up idea of traditional log-cabin construction, and is fitted with early 18th-century furniture.

On the river embankment in front is a curious memento brought from Manchuria in 1807: two mythical beasts that represent a remarkable cross-breeding of lion and frog.

Smolny

In mid-18th century a Baroque cathedral and convent was built by Rastrelli, beside the Neva River where it makes a hairpin bend north of the Alexander Nevsky Monastery. At first the convent buildings housed the Imperial Educational Society for Young Ladies. In 1809, this school for daughters of the nobility was rehoused alongside in the specially-built **Smolny Institute**.

Then came 1917. The Smolny Institute was taken over by the Bolsheviks, who used it as HQ of the October Revolution, from which Lenin directed the armed uprising. In Soviet political literature, Smolny is among the most famous place-names, where the historic events of October-November 1917 were enacted.

Smolny Institute today is not generally open to the public, as it remains the local Party HQ. A pleasant park avenue leads past a statue of Engels to the left, Marx to the right, and Lenin and the Smolny Institute straight ahead – an elegant building, with red flag flying.

The Cathedral and convent buildings are a blue-and-white fantasy. Although heavily damaged during the last war, this charming corner of Leningrad has been faithfully restored.

Piskarevskoye Memorial Cemetery

Many Intourist city tours end on a sombre note with a visit to the Memorial Cemetery where 470,000 citizens who died during the wartime siege are buried in mass graves. Out of the twenty million people lost by the Soviet Union during the war, 660,000 were from Leningrad.

Floral tributes are laid beneath a giant statue of Mother Russia. An inscription ends: 'No one has been forgotten, and nothing has been forgotten'.

3.4 Stroll Along Nevsky Prospekt

Not to be missed! Take a stroll along the most famous street in Russia. Planned in 18th century, the Nevsky Prospekt carves a three-mile swathe from the Admiralty to the Alexander Nevsky Monastery. Along Nevsky Prospekt, and in neighbouring squares and side streets, are located most of the city's principal shops and cinemas, and noble palaces, churches and bridges. All of Russia's giants of politics, literature and music have passed along this avenue which the Soviets carefully protect from the architectural ravages of the 20th century.

If you're going to shop-gaze (see section 3.7) or make sightseeing detours, three miles is a long way. The most rewarding section is from the Admiralty to Gostiny Dvor; and thence to Fontanka River. Alexander Nevsky Monastery is worth a separate trip. The avenue is well served by public transport – buses, trams, taxis or choice of four subway stations: Nevsky Prospekt, Gostiny Dvor, Mayakovskaya and Ploshchad Vosstaniya.

Let's start at the western end, by the Admiralty building with its slender golden spire. On the right, just past the Aeroflot terminus and a Beriozka store is Gogol Street, named after Nikolai Gogol who lived several years at No. 17, where he wrote *The Government Inspector* and part of *Dead Souls*. Tchaikovsky died at No. 13 Gogol Street.

After Gertsena Street on the right, at No. 15 is the **Barricada Cinema** which formerly was an 18th-century mansion that later became a Club for the Nobility.

On the opposite corner by the bridge over Moika River is the Literature Café, where one can have an afternoon glass of champagne, or make reservation for an evening meal. The atmosphere is charming, with chamber music recitals in a separate room from the restaurant, but still within earshot as background. As the 19th-century Café Wulf et Beranger, it was a favourite venue for the literary set in St Petersburg – Dostoevsky and the rest. From here, Pushkin left to fight the duel which led to his death. The poet lived close by, at No. 12 Moika Embankment.

Across the bridge on the corner of Nevsky Prospekt and Moika Embankment is the cheerful green and white baroque **Strogonov Palace** built by architect Rastrelli for the Count Stroganov family. Go through the archway into the pleasant central courtyard. The Stroganovs were famed for their rich art collection, which was re-housed after 1917 in the Hermitage. Today the family name is immortalized on restaurant menus, thanks to their favourite dish of boeuf.

The next major building, right, is **Kazan Cathedral** with colonnades sweeping round in two arms, somewhat like St Peter's in Rome. Unlike St Peter's, it is now a Museum of Religion and Atheism. Alongside is a pleasant

69

park, where Leningraders eat their midday sandwiches. Just look at the massive but decorative railings around the park. The Russian composer Glazunov lived down the street at No. 8 Ulitsa Plekhanova.

Beyond Kazan Cathedral is the Gribojedova Canal. Turn down to a delightful little bridge with a pair of golden-winged lions at each end. Then return to Nevsky Prospekt, where street photgraphers can now take your picture, sitting in what purports to be a vintage car.

The Metro subway station, Nevsky Prospekt, is on the opposite corner. The green and white building houses the **Maly Glinka Hall**, where many great musicians have performed.

Next is the Roman Catholic church of St Catherine, built 1764 in Baroque and Classical styles. Young Russian hippies and artists congregate there at evening time. If music calls, the Melodiya record shop is next door at No. 34. Stay on this side of Nevsky Prospekt if you want to make a sightseeing detour, left down Brodskovo Street, past Hotel Europe to Arts Square and the Russian Museum.

Opposite the Catholic Church is a State-run shop selling paintings and craft items – no bargains in sight! The colonnade in front is crammed easel-to-easel with young artists who do instant portraits.

At the next corner is **Gostiny Dvor** department store – the Merchants' Market – right by the subway. Even if you're not shop-minded, a visit is imperative. (More details, see section 3.7).

Opposite the Merchants' Bazaar is a beautiful blue-and-white **Armenian Church** which is protected as an architectural monument, but is not functioning. Neither is it a museum, so the entrance door remains padlocked.

Want to give your feet a rest? Try to find a seat in Café Sever, the café-restaurant with huge metal doors.

Switch back to the right-hand side of Nevsky Prospekt for sightseeing around **Ostrovsky Square**, designed by architect Rossi in the 1820's. On the first corner is the huge **Saltykov-Shchedrin Public Library**, one of the largest in the Soviet Union. Among its treasures is the book collection of Voltaire, bought by Catherine the Great. Tolstoy, Gorky and Lenin were regular readers at this Public Library.

Set back in Ostrovsky Square – named after the 19th-century Russian dramatist – is **Pushkin Theatre**, built 1832 by Rossi in Empire style. The Pushkin company, founded 1756, is the oldest in Russia. In the foreground park is a statue of Catherine the Second, surrounded by 18th-century VIPs.

Make a detour behind Pushkin Theatre, for the sightseeing bonus of **Rossi Street**, rated among the most elegant creations of architecture. The 22-metre building height is matched by the 22-metre street width. The building on the left is the **Theatre Museum** (open every afternoon except Tuesdays).

Next along Nevsky Prospekt, facing onto the Fontanka River, is **Anichkov Palace**, a handsome mid-18th century mansion of the Razumovsky's, used in 19th century as town house for heirs to the throne. With change of ownership, it's now the Zhdanov Palace of Young Pioneers, where thousands of young Leningraders every day attend hobby classes from sport to music, dancing and nature studies.

The **Anichkov Bridge** over the Fontanka River is famed for its four dramatic sculptures that represent the taming of wild horses. Across the river is the deep red Beloselsky-Belozersky Palace, built 1846–48 in imitation Baroque style.

Many people end their Nevsky Prospekt sightseeing here – perhaps switching to a canal boat tour from the pier by the bridge.

Otherwise, continue past several big cinemas to Uprising Square (Ploshchad Vosstanya, with a Metro) which commemorates the uprising of February 1917. The central obelisk is a memorial erected in 1985 to mark the 40th anniversary of the end of World War II. Across the square is Moscow Railway Station – an elegant green building, which couldn't look less like a railway terminus.

3.5   Take a Trip

The best excursions out of Leningrad are wrapped around visits to one or more of the great summer palaces of the tsars: at Pushkin and Pavlosk, which are near-enough neighbours to be combined into a single day-trip; and Petrodvorets.

Although these palaces were built as summer residences, a visit can still be delightful even in winter. You travel out through residential and industrial suburbs to open countryside. Sunshine glints on powdery snow that outlines the branch of every tree. It is supremely invigorating. Children skate on frozen ponds, while smaller children are hauled on sleds by their mothers.

The summertime view is equally attractive. Along the road to Pushkin are hundreds of acres of hot-houses, heated by natural gas and growing vegetables, mushrooms and salad crops. This district is a centre of agri-scientific studies, particularly around Pushkin town, where a number of scientific and research institutes have been transferred from central Leningrad.

In the woodlands are attractive wooden dachas, nestling amid the birch trees and surrounded by gardens heavily planted with vegetables, fruit trees and flowers. Guides explain that dachas are in private ownership, and can be bought or sold for around 5,000 roubles, which sounds remarkably cheap. The owners then pay about 25 roubles a year for use of the land. It's an interesting view of the Soviet life-style.

All this area saw years of bitter fighting during the 900-day wartime siege of Leningrad by Nazi troops, from September 1941 until early 1944. The front line, which ran only 4 miles from the outskirts of Leningrad, is marked by a memorial 'Green Belt of Glory'. A typical slogan on the city outskirts reads: 'Long live the Hero City of Leningrad!'.

Before their retreat, the Nazis thoroughly looted and blew up the three palaces. Rebuilding and restoration have steadily continued ever since, to salvage this part of the national heritage. In each palace, photographs show the original buildings, and a picture from 1944. The meticulous accuracy of restoration is quite incredible.

Very little furniture, for instance, survived the destruction. Replacements of suitable period and style were acquired from other museums and private collections. Copies were made by craftsmen who patiently followed the same traditions as their forebears. It's a slow process, with no modern short cuts permitted – all in the interests of authenticity.

Similar work has restored painted ceilings, elegant mirrors, panelled walls, rich wood-carving, gilded decorations, curtain materials, and parquet flooring. Typically, eight kilogrammes of gold were needed for the gilding of a single room in the Catherine Palace at Pushkin.

In each palace, tours are staggered with set hours for Intourist groups, who go through without waiting. Individuals pass through at other scheduled times. Large flight bags must be left in the cloakroom. Photography is OK, but no flash. To protect polished floors, everyone must wear canvas over-slippers. The flow of visitors is regulated by the number of slippers in stock, so there's never any overcrowding!

Pushkin

Following the wartime destruction, Pushkin town has been rebuilt, but with modern apartments in the centre. Originally the town was called Tsarskoe Selo – Royal Village. Because of proximity to the court, many wealthy Leningrad citizens built substantial summer houses. Russia's national poet, Alexander Pushkin, studied at the local secondary school for children of noble families.

After the Revolution, a number of mansions were converted to children's sanatoria, and the town was named Detskoye Selo – Children's Village. It was renamed Pushkin in 1937 to mark the 100th anniversary of the poet's death. Soviet tourists are specially interested in visiting buildings and monuments associated with his memory – particularly his old school, and a wing of the Catherine Palace which houses the All-Union Pushkin Museum. In a park there's a lovely statue of Pushkin sitting on his favourite bench.

Catherine Palace was built mid-18th century in most lavish Baroque style by the great Italian architect Rastrelli. This ultra-luxurious palace features the four elements of Russian Baroque: very rich woodcarving, painted ceilings, inlaid wood floors, and mirrors. Later alterations in classical style were made by a Scottish architect, Charles Cameron. The Cameron Gallery is considered to be the finest work of his five-year stint in Russia. The Palace grounds are laid out mainly in formal French style.

Pavlosk

This was a little present from Catherine the Great to her 22-year-old son, Paul – an elegant palace with 1300 acres. The style is a mixture of Baroque and Classical, designed by Charles Cameron, who also arranged the park layout. Most remarkable is the painted ceiling of the main dining room, which could easily deceive you into thinking it's dome-shaped, not flat. From almost total demolition in 1944, the entire reconstruction is superb.

Petrodvorets

Originally called Peterhof, this summer residence of Peter the Great was built on the shore of the Gulf of Finland in the early 18th century. It is 20 miles from central Leningrad. In 1715, work started on a fairly modest Grand Palace, which was then greatly enlarged in 1750 by Rastrelli. Wings and galleries were added to stretch in a yellow and white fantasy over an 850-ft frontage.

The Palace is famed for its Lower Park and Upper Garden, a-splash with 140 fountains. These culminate in the Grand Cascade with Samson pulling apart the jaws of a lion, who spurts a 65-ft water jet into the air. This celebrates a Russian victory over the Swedes on St Samson's Day in 1709.

In the overall park-and-palace complex, more living-space was available in the Monplaisir Palace, the Château de Marly and the Hermitage Pavilion.

3.6   Other Sights in Leningrad

After you have seen basic Leningrad and the summer palaces, and have strolled along Nevsky Prospekt, that's about the limit of what's possible on a brief city break. But if you still have any spare time, here are some suggestions on where else to go.

Boat Tour

There are several boat tour possibilities, though not in winter! A typical 75-minute circuit on the Neva River starts from a pier by the Winter Palace and costs one rouble, with commentary in fluent Russian. A five-mile circuit from the Anichkov Bridge on Nevsky Prospekt features mainly the Fontanka and Moyka Rivers.

Alexander Nevsky Monastery

Location: At furthest end of Nevsky Prospekt, by River Neva, opposite Hotel Moskva
Metro: Ploshchad Aleksandra Neskovo

One of Russia's most important monasteries, the Alexander Nevsky Lavra was founded in 1713 by Peter the Great.

After you pass through the entrance gate, the path is bordered by two walled cemeteries where many prominent Russians are buried. In the right-hand Tikhvin cemetery are numerous writers and musicians, including Dostoyevsky, Glinka, Mussorgsky, Borodin, Tchaikovsky and Rimsky-Korsakov.

The monastery buildings are used partly to house a **Museum of Town Sculpture**, open daily except Thursday from 11-18 hrs. Otherwise, this huge complex is a working monastery which is one of the best preserved buildings in Leningrad. Upkeep and decoration come entirely from church funds, with no State assistance. Seminary buildings are painted white and deep red, while the Cathedral of the Trinity is yellow ochre and white, with a golden steeple to the bell tower. Daily services are held at 10 a.m. in the Cathedral, with additional Saturday and Sunday services at 11.30 and 13 hrs.

Immediately opposite the church main entrance is the so-called Communist plot, where leading personalities of the last few decades are buried: ministers, commisars and many who died during the siege of Leningrad. One grave has an airplane propellor as its headstone. Others have a simple red star.

Museums & Galleries

Dostoyevsky Museum

Location: 5 Kuznechnyy Pereulok – past the covered market behind Vladimirskaya Metro station, at corner of Dostoyevsky Street
Open: daily except Monday, 10.30-18.30

The Dostoyevsky family lived in the 2nd-floor flat from October 1878 until the writer died in 1881. Exhibited are many personal belongings of the Dostoyevsky's, with authentic furniture, giving a good idea of the life-style of one of Russia's greatest writers. He wrote his novel *The Brothers Karamazov* in the well-equipped study, four rooms' distant from the clamour of the nursery. In the floor above, several rooms show the development of the author's literary life.

Pushkin Museum

Location: 12 Moyka River Embankment, close to Nevsky Prospekt
Open: daily except Tuesday, 11-18 hrs.
Pushkin lived here in the final months before he was killed in a duel with his sister-in-law's husband, Baron d'Anthès. Rooms are furnished as in Pushkin's day, with a collection of his personal belongings.

History of Leningrad Museum

Location: 44 Naberezhnaya Krasnogo Flota (Red Fleet Embankment) past Lt. Schmidt Bridge
Open: Thursday and Saturday 11-17 hrs; Tuesday and Sunday 11-16 hrs; Friday and Monday 13-19 hrs. Closed Wednesdays.
Covers the city's history from foundation until today, including a special section on the 900-day wartime siege.

Lenin Museum

Location: 5/1 Ulitsa Khalturina (by Kirov Bridge, facing Field of Mars)
Open: daily except Wednesday 10.30-18.30
Housed in the pale pink Marble Palace built 1785, the Museum features a rich cross-section of Lenin's activities. In the courtyard is the armoured car from which Lenin made his first speech when he arrived in April 1917 at the Finland Station. Quite apart from the political interest, the palace itself is worth visiting for its lavish decoration with 32 different kinds of marble.

October Revolution Museum

Location: 4 Ulitsa Kuibysheva (close to Peter and Paul Fortress and the Cruiser Aurora)
Open: Monday and Friday 14-19 hrs; Tuesday, Wednesday, Saturday, Sunday 11-19 hrs. Closed Thursday.
Originally the town house of a famed ballerina, the building was used as a Bolshevik Party HQ in 1917. From the balcony, Lenin made political speeches. The museum documents the period leading to the October Revolution, and contains works by Soviet painters and sculptors. Historic films are shown in the Museum's cinema.

3.7 Go Shopping in Leningrad

Beriozka shops

The principal hotels have these hard-currency shops with a limited choice of souvenir items. (Plaintive cry from a tourist, faced with a single counter: 'Is *that* the whole store?') The largest Beriozka is at 9 Nevksy Prospekt – top end, near the Admiralty. Home in on the Aeroflot sign. It's certainly worth a visit, offering a full range of Soviet jewellery, watches, cameras, wooden toys and souvenirs, fur hats and coats, gramophone records, art books, perfumes, Soviet and imported drinks and cigarettes, Havana cigars and musical instruments.

There's another Beriozka quite close at 26 Ulitsa Gertsena (Hertzen Street) on the corner of Dzerzhinskovo Street.

Nevksy Prospekt

To try and spend roubles, best policy is to concentrate on Nevsky Prospekt. See section 3.4 for combining shop-gazing with sightseeing. If your heart is set on specific products like books, revolutionary posters or gramophone records, save time by going direct to Dom Knigi (House of Books) at 28 Nevsky Prospekt – a landmark building with a glass globe on top, from the days when the building belonged to the Singer Sewing Machine Company. Further along, at no. 34, is Melodiya, with enormous choice of low-cost gramophone records. Try no. 54 for antiques. At no. 48 is Passage, a large department store. By the corner of Ulitsa Zhelabova, near no. 22, is the DLT Department Store, one of the largest in Leningrad.

Otherwise, for general browsing, you can't beat a visit to the **Gostiny Dvor** at 35 Nevsky Prospekt. This 'Merchants Yard' dates from 1785. It's an extraordinary, rambling department store, composed of hundreds of small stalls and counters, jumbled around the galleries of a rambling square building. Going from one haphazard counter to another, you get a general overview of Soviet consumer products. (Metro: Gostiny Dvor; or Nevsky Prospekt.)

Equally interesting is to peek into the numerous food stores along Nevsky Prospekt – dairy products, fish, meat, sausage-shops, confectioners, bakers. Mostly they are walled, floor to ceiling, with white tiles, and lit by elegant chandeliers. How often do you see chandeliers in your home-town fish shops? Some stores seem ultra-hygienic, with a strong background of disinfectant.

Often, a window display is just a pot plant or a lace curtain. The foreign visitor has little clue about what's being sold inside, unless he can decipher the Russian fascia-board. Just walk in, and look! A typical empty window proclaimed the sale of wines, champagne and cognac. Inside, all they had was boxes of matches, and

bottles of vodka costing 10 roubles, with customers'
queuing to get lit up.

A Farmer's Market

For more basic interest, it's worth visiting a fruit, flower
and vegetable market where private-sector produce is
sold. There's a good one at Kuznechny Lane, just behind
Vladimirskaya Metro station (three stops from Ploshchad
Lenina which serves Leningrad Hotel); or you can reach it
by walking 400 yards down Vladimirsky Prospekt which
turns south off Nevsky Prospekt.

Outside the covered market, women sell knitted hats,
flowers and vegetables. Inside, it's very hygienic and tiled –
an architect-designed market from the mid-1920's with a
flavour of Baroque. Peasants offer a full range of food
products, including honey, cottage cheese, soft fruits and
well-polished tomatoes. Some prices are rather unnerving,
particularly for exotic fruits which have been flown up
from the warm south.

Appropriately, at the Metro station there's a huge
mosaic at the escalator entrance, depicting an idealised
country scene of peasants' glowing with riches from the
harvest.

Just past the covered market, at the first right-hand
corner down Kuznechny Lane, is the Dostoyevsky House
Museum at no. 5. (See section 3.6.)

3.8   Eating Out in Leningrad

Make a reservation through Intourist or your tour
operator representative. Otherwise you could wait till
tomorrow for a table to come free. Here's a recommended
short list of top-grade Leningrad restaurants:

Sadko, Nevsky Prospekt, corner of Ulitsa Brodskovo,
next to Hotel Europe
Russian style cuisine, rated the best in Leningrad, with
dancing to a balalaika orchestra Try their Georgian wines,
Soviet champagne and caviar. Finish up with chocolate ice
cream.

Baku, Ulitsa Sadovaya 12 (close to Gostiny Dvor
department store)
Azerbaijan dishes – spicy Caucasian food with good
bread. Try their satsivi cold appetiser, basturma type of
shish kebab, and cold coffee with ice cream.

Kavkazky (the Caucasian), 25 Nevsky Prospekt
Caucasian food including Kharcho soup (somewhat like

gazpacho), shashlik, tabaka chicken, and cherbureki
(mutton and rice cakes). There's a downstairs band, or
you can choose a quieter meal on the ground floor.

3.9   Leningrad by Night

Russian music, ballet and opera are famous throughout
the world, and no one should miss a visit to at least one
theatre during a stay in Leningrad. Intourist can advise on
programmes, and reserve tickets. Those in search of
culture are particularly drawn to Leningrad for the
renowned White Nights Festival (every year, June 21–29)
featuring classical ballet and folk dances.

Evening theatre and circus shows begin at 7.30 p.m.;
matinees at 11 a.m. Concerts start at 8 p.m.

Among the city's 17 theatres are the following:

Kirov Opera and Ballet, 1 Teatrainaya Ploshchad
(Theatre Square)

Also known as the Mariya, the world-famous Kirov has
launched the greatest international stars such as Anna
Pavlova, Nijinsky and Ulanova; Rudolf Nureyev, Mikhail
Baryshnikov and Natalia Makarova; and Chaliapin among
the singers. It saw the world premiers of Verdi's *La Forza
del Destino* as well as Tchaikovsky's *Sleeping Beauty*,
Nutcracker, and most of the great Russian operas.

Maly Theatre of Opera and Ballet, 1 Ploshchad
Iskusstv

If you cannot make the Kirov, the Maly is a first-class
second choice! The name means 'small', but there's seating
for 1200. The present building dates from mid-19th
century.

Pushkin Theatre and Theatre of Comedy, Ploshchad
Ostrovskovo

Russia's oldest dramatic theatre, the Pushkin is located
on Ostrovskovo Square, near Gostinny Dvor on Nevsky
Prospekt.

Philharmonic Concert Hall
This is the home of the Leningrad Symphony Orchestra.
The Grand Hall is located at 2 Ulitsa Brodskogo; the Small
Hall at 30 Nevsky Prospekt.

Oktyabrsky Grand Concert Hall, 6 Ligovskiy Prospekt
Close to Moscow Station (Metro: Vosstaniya Ploschchad),
this is one of Russia's largest concert halls, with 4,000
capacity. It features symphony concerts, theatrical
productions and folk-music productions.

Leningrad State Circus
The main arena is on Naberezhnaya Fontanki; the summer arena is on Moskovsky Prospekt.

Excellent folk-dancing performances are sometimes given in a splendid auditorium at the Leningrad Hotel.